Little Red Book
of
Modern Writing Skills

By the same author

Little Red Book Series

Little Red Book of SMS Slang and Chat Room Slang	Little Red Book of Synonyms
Little Red Book of English Vocabulary Today	Little Red Book of Antonyms
Little Red Book of Grammar Made Easy	Little Red Book of Common Errors
Little Red Book of English Proverbs	Little Red Book of Letter Writing
Little Red Book of Prepositions	Little Red Book of Essay Writing
Little Red Book of Idioms and Phrases	Little Red Book of Word Fact
Little Red Book of Effective Speaking Skills	Little Red Book of Spelling
Little Red Book of Phrasal Verbs	Little Red Book of Language Checklist
Little Red Book of Euphemisms	Little Red Book of Perfect Written English
Little Red Book of Word Power	Little Red Book of Punctuation
	Little Red Book of Reading and Listening Skills
	Little Red Book of A Child's First Dictionary

A2Z Book Series

A2Z Quiz Book	A2Z Book of Word Origins

Others

The Book of Fun Facts The Book of More Fun Facts The Book of Firsts and Lasts The Book of Virtues Word Fact Finder	The Book of Motivation Read Write Right: Common Errors in English The Students' Companion
Fun Facts: Science Fun Facts: Animals Fun Facts: India Fun Facts: Nature	Fun with Maths Fun with Numbers Fun with Puzzles Fun with Riddles

Little Red Book *of* Modern Writing Skills

Terry O'Brien

RUPA

Published by
Rupa Publications India Pvt. Ltd 2011
7/16, Ansari Road, Daryaganj
New Delhi 110002

Sales centres:
Prayagraj Bengaluru Chennai
Hyderabad Jaipur Kathmandu
Kolkata Mumbai

Copyright © Terry O'Brien 2011

All rights reserved.
No part of this publication may be reproduced, transmitted,
or stored in a retrieval system, in any form or by any means,
electronic, mechanical, photocopying, recording or otherwise,
without the prior permission of the publisher.

ISBN: 978-81-291-1851-6

Eleventh impression 2023

15 14 13 12 11

The moral right of the author has been asserted.

Typeset by Innovative Processors, New Delhi

Printed in India

This book is sold subject to the condition that it shall not, by way of trade
or otherwise, be lent, resold, hired out, or otherwise circulated, without
the publisher's prior consent, in any form of binding or cover other than
that in which it is published.

I dedicate this book to late Prof. A.P. O'Brien, my father, friend, guide and mentor, who inspired me to the canon of excellence: re-imagining what's essential

PREFACE

English writing skills include formal and informal style, résumés, cover letters, and other business documents, essays and much more. Learning is a skill and it can be improved.

In this age where communication is the key, few skills are more important for a person to master than writing. If you don't think you're a good writer or would like to become a better one, there are plenty of things you can do to improve your writing. *Little Red Book of Modern Writing Skills* gives some ways how you can hone your writing skills and become better at communicating via the written word.

1. **Write every day.** If you want to be a better writer, write more. Write every day if possible—even a journal entry, an email or a letter will do. The best way to develop effective writing skills is to practice, practice, practice.
2. **Read--a lot!** Reading offers writers a lot of benefits: you see how great writers construct their work: Style, diction, construction of sentences, paragraphs, whole pieces. Reading helps you expand your vocabulary. Often, even simple articles or stories contain new words or terms that you can tuck away for your own future use. Reading expands the world you know about—the more you know, the more fodder you have for writing of any kind. If you want to be a good writer, be a good reader.

3. **Commit certain basic rules to memory and force yourself to use them: 3 R's: Read, Record, Recall.** While many of the minute peculiarities of grammar may not come into play everyday, the basic grammar and writing skills do. And one way to develop writing skills is to learn these basics and make sure you use them all the time. The person who has a run-on sentence, writes in fragments, or throws in random commas all the time, will not have the same success as a writer who knows the basics.

Good writers should know how to write short, concise, complete sentences. They should know when to use commas to separate ideas in a sentence—and when not to do so. They should know how to get a subject and verb to agree. They should know how to use pronouns clearly. And they should know the difference between jargon and real words.

Little Red Book of Modern Writing Skills will help you know the basics that can help your writing to improve. And once you have the basics, you can go on acquiring more skills.

Wishing you great success!

Best of luck!

Terry O'Brien

The Modern Writer: Quills to Skills

Today, when we think of writing, the image of a man sitting in front of his desk with sheets of paper before him, a pen in his hand and an inkwell on the table, rarely comes to mind. But that was how writers practiced their craft in the olden days. In those days, the only tools a writer needed were an imaginative and creative mind, a powerful vocabulary, flair and passion for writing, a pen and sheets of paper.

Quill was the writing instrument that dominated the early years of writing – for more than 1400 years. Even now, some calligraphers use quill pens for their craft. Later, the quill was replaced by the fountain pen. Lewis Waterman invented the fountain pen and got a patent for it in 1884. With the invention of fountain pens writers could spend more time thinking and writing rather than preparing their writing instruments and inks. The ballpoint pen made its appearance in 1938; it was invented by Laszlo Biro, a journalist from Hungary. The writing instruments continued to evolve and got better thus making writing less cumbersome. But the power of the words still remains unchanged and the pen still plays a crucial role in shaping and changing the history of mankind and the lives of many.

Writers inspire, motivate, inform, engage, excite, empower, and take their readers through a range of emotions from absolute bliss to utter dismay with their words. Wars start and end, treaties and pacts get signed, people become famous or notorious, heroes are praised and villains punished, courtships start, love bloom and blossom, lovers get married, and some marriages end in divorces, authors are born and influence generations, people gossip, spy on each other, countries flourish and perish, all at the stroke of the pen.

Prophet Muhammad (Peace Be Upon Him) is quoted as saying "The ink of the scholar is holier than the blood of the martyr."

It was in 1839, the English author Edward Bulwer-Lytton coined the adage "The pen is mightier than the sword." This is undoubtedly the Truth.

The power of words cannot be overemphasised. According to Lord Byron: "Words are things; and a small drop of ink, Falling like dew upon a thought, Produces that which makes thousands, perhaps millions think."

Writers should master the words and should learn everything that will make their writing more accurate, effective, captivating, attractive, and influential.

The modern writers need all the skills their predecessors possessed. The skills remain the same - an imaginative and creative mind, powerful vocabulary, and flair and passion for writing.

But the tools have changed. The quill got replaced by the pen long time back. Now even the pen is slowly being replaced by computers.

It is true once a new technology rolls over you, if you are not part of the steamroller, you are not part of the road. This is very true in the case of computers and information technology. In today's information age, knowledge of computers is a must. We use computers, either directly or indirectly, in each and every aspect of our lives. We use computers on many different occasions in our day-to-day life. Computers, Internet, and Information Technology (IT) are changing the way writers write, copy-editors edit, reviewers review, and even readers read.

Today an author can publish what he has written in a matter of seconds. He can upload it to his blog, which will be read by people all over the world who can comment about the article, recommend it to friends, and so on. All this can happen in a matter of minutes. Writers can work from anywhere in the world and the audience is the entire world. The canvas is immense; the dimensions are varied.

Every Word Counts

Vigorous writing is concise. A sentence should contain no unnecessary words, a paragraph no unnecessary sentences, for the same reason that a drawing should have no unnecessary lines and a machine no unnecessary parts. This does not mean that the writer makes all the sentences short, or that he avoids all detail and treats his subject only in outline, but that every word tells.

Writing is a talent which, if not difficult to develop, needs time, patience and **special techniques** to develop and master. One can enhance this skill by continuously **writing** as practice can do it all. Whether **writing** a blog or a business letter, an email or an essay, the prime goal should be to counter directly and evidently to the requirements and interests of the audience one is addressing to.

Writing well can be divided into many types. There is creative writing, writing in the workplace, academic writing, professional copywriting and the list goes on. But the basics are the same for all kinds and types of writing. If you set them well, then nobody can stop you from being a good writer.

The skills of writing can be grasped by following a **few basic tips** to help you enhance your writing skills as it is important to have a command over the **language** as well as the **editing techniques.** Writing alone does not do it all. What is more important is to have the talent to re-write.

MULTUM IN PARVO: Much in Less

You can write but can you write well? A good writer is like a sculptor. They continually use less and less to express more and more. A sculptor takes a mound of clay as the medium and cuts away to get form and beauty. Similarly, a good writer cuts away useless words and makes every word count. In writing, as in all art the canon is: *Multum in parvo*: less is more. 'Only the hand that erases can write the true thing'. Correct sentences are written; good sentences are often re-written.

Here are **Dos** and **Don'ts** for effective writing: Be simple. Have clarity. Brevity is the soul of wit. Let us use our words the way we spend our money. Learning to write is learning to think.

1. Try to use picture words rather than abstract words, e.g. 'bus', 'car' or 'train' rather than 'vehicle', a 'cat' or a 'dog' rather than an 'animal'.
2. Write less, say more: Use one-syllable words rather than two-syllable words, two-syllable words rather than three, etc. Example: 'blood, tears, sweat, toil' rather than 'sacrifice, sorrow, perspiration, effort'. Why write 'subsequently'; write 'later'. Not more than 25 percent of your words should have more than two syllables. Prefer vivid pictures to abstract words.

3. Use the active voice rather than the passive (not: 'The bicycle was fixed by me', but: 'I fixed the bicycle'). Write as you talk.
4. Verbs words that denote action in every sentence. Choose strong graphic verbs, e.g. 'Shahrukh *struggled* with the problem for days'. If you choose the effective verb then an adverb is not needed.
5. Each word counts. Don't use two words where one can do the needful.
6. Sentences should generally be less than 18 words; vary their length as a good bowler varies his length. Keep clauses short. 18 is the danger alarm!
7. One paragraph, one idea. Clear writing comes from clear thinking. You don't know anything clearly, unless you can state it in writing.
8. Relate to the experience of your audience; e.g., if for computer buffs, then your writing should be filled with hardware, software, data entry, input and output etc.
9. Write not to ***IM-press*** but to ***EX-press.***
10. The reader loses interest quickly. To hold him/her be as personal as the situation allows, by using personal pronouns (I, you, she, etc.), questions to the reader, exclamations. Involve the reader to be with you within the lines and even read between the lines.
11. Writing is hard work: exert yourself. 'I think, therefore, I AM' said Descartes. Indeed, writing is a form of therapy: Good sentences are not written, they are simply re-written.
12. Words move, music moves. Every language has its own music. Read your work aloud to see whether it has the correct 'feel'. Sound does come before sense as we know in from our kindergarten days.

Ten Rules for Brevity Writing

1. It is what you make of a story not the story itself.
2. Never summarise without reason.
3. Conduct an inquiry.
4. Consider the unique, the nuances, not the commonly known.
5. Use your experiences.
6. Develop your own voice.
7. Offer a point of view.
8. Think about craft: is the writing too loose or written without sufficient concentration?
9. Consider the Critical Thinking rubric.
10. Risk something.

The Importance of Brevity

The purpose of writing is to communicate a particular message. It is harder to be brief with this message than it is to write a lengthy piece. This is because we want to communicate all of our ideas into one spot. The point of brevity is not just to say less, but to communicate a message more concisely. By deleting needless words or sentences and editing, this is possible.

Important questions to answer: *Can it be better? Can it make more sense? What details could I leave out? Can I restructure my sentences?*

Trim the Matter – Remove the Unnecessary load

The tighter the message, the easier readers get roped in. So it is important to make every word tell part of the story.

Eliminate words

Avoid superfluous nouns, verbs, articles, prepositions- that obscure meaning rather than clarify it. Avoid "the fact that," "who is" and "which was": these are the most commonly used needless words. Here are a few more examples:

- "the field of technology" and "the technology industry" BECOME "technology"
- "the amount of total sales increased" BECOMES "sales increased"
- "have a tendency to" BECOMES "tend to"
- "are going to" BECOMES "will"
- "some of the people" BECOMES "some people"
- "I am writing in regards to" BECOMES "I'm writing about"

Choose your words carefully

Choose concrete, precise, everyday terms to those less specific and familiar is a way to do this:

- "organisation" BECOMES "group"
- "utilise" or "utilisation" BECOMES "use"
- "morbidity" or "mortality" BECOMES "illness" or "death"
- "interface with each other" BECOMES "collaborate"

Use active voice

This helps to make every word tell, verses a passive voice, which is more verbose and less dynamic.

- "The class was taught by me" BECOMES "I taught the class"

- "This is the first time that institution has enrolled any female students" BECOMES "Women will attend that institution for the first time this session"

"There's a lot of support of the proposition" BECOMES "Many people support the proposition"

Write First, Edit Later

Don't worry about writing concisely on the first try. Go back later and make edits. Your first read will tell you words or sentences that sound redundant or don't make sense. Then go back and make more edits. And while brevity is important, so is clarity. If your piece is brief, but not clear, then the purpose is defeated. When you get brevity right, you can say more with less number of words.

Once more: Less is more

It doesn't matter whether you are talking (or writing) about words, phrases, sentences, paragraphs, memos, letters or reports. Less is more!

Words:

Not	But
Subsequently	later
Forward	send
Reveal	show
Modification	change

Phrases:

Not	But
basic fundamentals	fundamentals
assemble together	assemble
at an early date	soon
held a meeting with	met

Sentences:

Not	But
What is the receptivity of the organisation to change	Can the organisation change?
Business failure itself is an everyday occurrence in our country	Business fail in India daily

Writing in the World Around us Today

We live in **a world where screens dominate** our time.

- Lots of us sleep with our phones by the bed. (Some will admit to keeping them right under the pillow.)
- We check e-mail while we're still yawning.
- Our web browser usually has more than four tabs open. Notifications and distractions come to us all day long.
- We have hundreds of TV channels and a few multiplex theaters nearby.
- We also have YouTube, where every minute another 24 hours of content is uploaded.

We are undoubtedly facing an all-out war on our attention.

Here are some **ways you can win** it. They all involve **brevity.**

In Writing

- Keep your sentences compact. People don't have time to dissect your flowery prose, especially in business.
- Short, punchy sentences help people stay on target with you.

On Twitter

- Make your stuff easier to re-tweet.
- Twitter has a 140-character limit. If you use only 110 or so, you'll give people room to re-tweet to you and thus spread your message even further.

Via e-mail

Folks living on Facebook, e-mail messages need to fit into a smaller package. Two hundred words should be the max.

- *NOTE*: If you need more, then it's a document, not an e-mail—or it's a phone call or even a face-to-face visit.
- Do put the actionable part at the top once, and at the bottom a second time. We're all scanning.

On YouTube

- No matter which video platform you use, make your videos two minutes or less, on average.
- Yes, if it's a speech—it should be longer. But if it's something you want people to take home, stay under two minutes.

By Phone

- Should you still use a telephone, keep the call brief. Start with an agenda, even if you don't state it out loud.

- Write it down beforehand so you don't ramble.
- Be polite, but don't waste five minutes on small talk.

By Voice Mail

- Leave your full name, phone number and the subject of the call.
- Say your number once more before hanging up.

Write To Speak

Good working language – a skill you can learn.

Brevity is the soul of wit: Clear, complete

Keep your language lively: Avoid habitual use of the passive

Do not voice, unnecessary words and vague: And illumination was called for by a supreme being *rather*

And God said, Let there be light

The more you write, more fluent your writing will become

ABC of Writing

Accuracy, Brevity, Clarity

Try to keep a Paragraph: short – 5/6 lines sentences

Complaining	Tell why you are writing
Of a product	Give the product
Where you bought it	What you want/desire
Model no.	…………….

Good Usage for Good Communication

Correct Usage

Colloquial usage sometimes tends to disregard strict grammatical rules.

Best e.g. is "me" instead of "I".

Who is it? We answer "It's me".

It's I – wrong in strictly Grammar terms – But no one bothers.

But in written English – "It is I who am responsible for this department";

Not 'It is me'

Usage – of course involves something more than basic grammar – often depends on the sense and the meaning of the word liable – likely:

"Leave me alone" usage written "Let me alone".

Circumlocution

This is circumlocution – to write something in a long winded way:

'The fact that one acts in a hasty manner is bound to result in an inefficient use of one's time or goods'.

Simply this is what one wants to state: *'Haste makes waste'*

Grammar and Usage

- Dull rules and duller drills.
- Yet grammar, with a precise vocabulary and proper usage – keys to good writing.
- Grammar – quality of game.

- Split a sentence, take it apart, then put it together – a jigsaw puzzle.
- Pieces of the grammar are parts of speech.
- Put the pieces together to form a recognisable picture.
- Children become like detectives discovering the relationship between words and phrases and clauses.

Creative Writing

Creative writing is anything where the purpose is to express thoughts, feelings and emotions rather than to simply convey information. Creative fiction (Short stories and novels), poetry, autobiography, biography and creative non-fiction are all forms of creative writing.

Creative writing is writing that expresses the writer's thoughts and feelings in an imaginative, often unique, and poetic way. However, writing is a form of personal freedom. Ogden Nash the poet thus wrote:

"In comparison with men of golden talents,
I am all a man of talent ought to be;
I resemble every genius in his vice, however heinous -
Yet I write so much like me."

Writing of any sort is hard, but rewarding work – you'll gain a huge amount of satisfaction from a finished piece.

Being creative can also be difficult and challenging at times, but immensely fun. And if you end gazing at a blank screen for hours, try kick starting your writing with a short exercise. Don't stop to think too much about it … just get going, without worrying about the quality of the work you produce.

Tips for Beginners

- **Do some short exercises to stretch your writing muscles**
  Try to get into the habit of writing every day, even if it's just for ten minutes.
- **If you're stuck for ideas, carry a notebook everywhere and write down your observations.** You'll get some great lines of dialogue by keeping your ears open on the bus or in cafes or a railway train, and an unusual phrase may be prompted by something you see or smell.
- **Work out the time of day when you're at your most creative.** For many writers, this is first thing in the morning – before all the demands of the day jostle for attention. Others write well late at night, after the rest of the members of the family have gone to bed. Don't be afraid to experiment!
- **Don't agonise over getting it right.** All writers have to revise and edit their work – it's rare that a story, scene or even a sentence comes out perfectly the first time. Once you've completed the initial draft, leave the piece for a few days – then come back to it fresh, with a red pen in hand.
- **HAVE FUN!** Sometimes, we writers can end up feeling that our writing is a chore, something that "must" be done, or something to procrastinate over for as long as possible. If your plot seems wildly far-fetched, your characters bore you to tears and you're convinced that a five-year old with a crayon could write better prose … take a break. Start a completely new project, something which is purely for fun. Write a poem or a 50-word "mini saga". Just completing a small finished piece can help if you're bogged down in a longer story.

Creative Writing Tips

Creative Writing Tip #1: Figurative Language

Figurative Speech uses language in original, imaginative ways to create strong images. Two common figures of speech are similes and metaphors.

A **Simile** explicitly compares one thing to another, using the word *like* or *as*; as in:

Sharp as flint...solitary as an oyster.

A **Metaphor** is a figure of speech that implies a comparison by speaking of one thing as if it were another, without using the word *like* or *as*:

*Why, what a **candy deal** of courtesy*

Creative Writing Tip #2: Strong Action Verbs

Write with strong action verbs. Active verbs are dynamic; passive verbs are insipid.

Active Verb: Allen caught the lion.
Passive Verb: The lion was caught by Allen.

An action verb electrifies. Active verbs are vivid verbs; they evoke drama and suspense, they rivet the reader's attention.

Creative Writing Tip #3: Denotations

Good word-choice is important. Readers expect words to be used according to their **denotations**: that is, their established dictionary definitions.

Some words may have the same general definitions. For example: *famous, noted, renowned, celebrated, talked-about* and *notorious* all mean *widely-known*. But each of these words carries a different denotation.

Choose words that precisely fit your meaning. A *celebrated* author is very different from a *notorious* one. Wrong choice of words weakens your writing and confuses readers.

Consult a good dictionary if you're unsure of the precise meaning of a word.

Creative Writing Tip #4: Connotations

Words also have **connotations**: emotional overtones that go beyond the word's explicit definition. When choosing words, be sensitive to their connotations.

Explore the overtones in different words. Words with approximately similar meanings may have different connotations. For example, each of these words evokes an entirely different response from the reader: *fat, plump, chubby, pot-bellied, paunchy, obese.*

Emotional associations add layers of meaning to your writing. Sentences are especially potent when constructed with emotionally charged words, because of the rich interplay of connotations among the words.

If you're unsure of the connotation of a word, consult a good dictionary of synonyms.

Creative Writing Tip #5: Concrete Words

Balance general words and abstract ideas with **specific** and **concrete** words.

General words name groups of things: for example, *fish, fruit*. Abstract words name qualities or ideas: for example, *protection, danger*. Specific and concrete words name things that appeal to our senses of sight, hearing, touch, taste or smell: for example, *cat, orange, park*.

General and abstract words paint a broad but sketchy picture. Use them to set out your main idea, then flesh them out with specific and concrete words that evoke vivid images in the minds of readers.

Creative Writing Tip #6: Show, Don't Tell

Get readers involved in your story, make them feel *with* and *for* your characters. One way of doing this is to show characters' feelings and personalities through action and dialogue.

Creative Writing Tip #7: Word Music

When we read, we hear the words with our inner ear. The way an author writes, especially the interplay of word choice, syntax and repetition, determines the way the words sound to readers: whether it's discord or melody that they hear. Good writing has a musical rhythm to it. Charles Dickens draws us into *A Tale of Two Cities* with this lyrical opening:

It was the best of times, it was the worst of times, it was the age of wisdom, it was the age of foolishness, it was the epoch of belief, it was the epoch of incredulity, it was the season of Light, it was the season of Darkness, it was the spring of hope, it was the winter of despair...

And the poignant, triumphant note on which the story ends: listen as the stirring music draws to a close:

"It is a far, far better thing that I do, than I have ever done; it is a far, far better rest that I go to, than I have ever known."

(From *A Tale of Two Cities*, by Charles Dickens)

Create Word Music with Onomatopoeia, Alliteration, Repetition & More

What is *word music*? It's the music our inner ear "hears", even as our eyes read the words on a page.

The way an author writes - the interplay of word choice, voice and syntax - influences the word music the reader hears. Good writers choose and arrange words in rhythmical patterns to reflect a mood or arouse emotions in the reader.

As you write, listen with your inner ear; or, better still, read your work aloud. Does your writing flow smoothly or does it sound as though you've got pebbles in your mouth? Does the word music echo or enhance your theme, or detract from it?

Tips to Create the Music of Words

Create Word Music with Onomatopoeia

Onomatopoeic words imitate the sounds, movements or feelings they describe; for example: *murmur, babble, clang, mumble, moan, drone, buzz, hiss, sigh, ooze, churn, crack, quiver, rustle, shiver, sizzle, flicker, whirl, twirl, tumble, swoon*.

Onomatopoeia creates musical effects and brings images to life.

Create Word Music with Alliteration

This is when the same sound gets repeated in several words running close together; it can be a loud plosive, as in *batter, bash, bang, bump, battle, bomb*; or a softer, muted note as in *mummy, milk, mellow, melody, moon, murmur*.

Alliteration helps to convey meaning and mood: contrast the explosive force of *Don't do it!; Drop dead!; Down, Doggy, down!* with the mellower tones in *mummy's milk; merry melody; marry me*; or the light, lingering effect created by the *l* consonants.

Alliteration: the repetition of the same sound at the beginning of a word, such as the repetition of b sounds in Keats's "beaded bubbles winking at the brim" ("Ode to a Nightingale") or the 'm' sound in Coleridge's "Five miles meandering in a mazy motion ("Kubla Khan"). A common use for alliteration is emphasis. It occurs in everyday speech in such phrases as "tittle-tattle," "bag and baggage," "bed and board," "primrose path," and "through thick and thin" and in sayings like "look before you leap."

Create Word Music with Vowel Sounds

Writers use vowel sounds to reveal moods and emotions. Quick, lilting *i* and *e* vowels create a light-hearted feeling, while long vowels and diphthongs like *a, o, u* and *ea* sound rich and warm, as in this example:

> *My love is like a red, red rose*
>
> *or*
>
> In Xanadu did Kubla Khan
> A stately pleasure dome decree:
> Where Alph, the sacred river, ran
> Through caverns measureless to man
> Down to a sunless sea

Rich, full vowels also evoke a sense of abundance.

Create Word Music with Assonance

Assonance is the repetition of similar vowel sounds close together, as in *The rain in Spain falls mainly on the plain*.

This repetition reinforces mood and feeling, and gives unity to sentences. Examples: for a touch of warm humour, as in *how now, brown cow?*; for a lighthearted, hopeful tone, as in *star light, star bright, first star I see tonight*; or to evoke a sense of awe, as in *O Lord my God, when I in awesome wonder, consider all the worlds...*

Writers also use assonance to create word music with a rhythmical beat to it.

Create Word Music with Resonance

Resonance is a prolonged, vibrating sound that adds fullness and weight to words. It is useful for recreating the din and bustle of a crowd, droning voices or background noises. Resonance of the *m*, *n* and *ng* sounds are found in these lines:

The moan of doves in immemorial elms,
And murmur of innumerable bees.

Create Word Music with Repetition

Repetition is especially effective in children's stories. Kids love jingles and repetitive rhymes; in fact they need this repetition to learn words. Studies have shown that constant reiteration improves a child's flow of language; think, for example, of nursery rhymes like *Mary Had a Little Lamb* and favourite tales like *The Three Little Pigs* ("Then I'll huff and I'll puff, and I'll blow your house down") and *Jack and the Beanstalk* ("Fie Fee Fo Fum, I smell the blood of an Englishman")

Repetition builds emotion to a peak. Feel the throb and swell of the word music as it rises to a crescendo, in these last moving words at the close of *A Tale of Two Cities*:

It is a far, far better thing that I do, than I have ever done; it is a far, far better rest that I go to, than I have ever known."

How to Improve Writing Skills

Creative Writing Tip #1: Be Simple

Write in the simple, natural language of everyday speech. This doesn't mean that you confine yourself to only the most basic words, but that you avoid pompous language, which may cloud your meaning or send readers to sleep.

For example, do not say, *He acquired an instrument of destruction wherewith he decapitated the formidable foe*, when you mean, *with his axe he chopped off the giant's head*. Use short, familiar words rather than long, obscure ones - unless the longer word fits your meaning more precisely.

Most good writing is simple. Read the Bible. Simple language is the strongest and most effective. The shortest sentence in the Bible has just two words: "Jesus wept".

One way to acquire good style is to study the works of great writers: not to imitate them but to learn how simple language can be elegant, lyrical and powerful.

Creative Writing Tip #2: Be Yourself

Be yourself; be natural and sincere. Don't try to imitate another writer's style; find your own, the style that bears the stamp of your personality.

A guarded, polished style is like a faceless mask; it's not real. Good writing resonates with the true voice of the human author, with all of that author's warmth, wit, idiosyncrasies and vulnerabilities.

Write as if you're speaking to a friend. Your reader should be able to hear the rhythms and cadences of your speaking voice. Your family and friends should be able to say, "This sounds like you."

Creative Writing Tip #3: Be Precise

Choose words that say precisely what you mean.

Avoid trite words like *nice, interesting, big*. As in: *We had a nice dinner; That's a big bird*. Be specific. Is it *sushi, wonton* or *mutton curry*? Is it *a flamingo, an eagle* or *an ostrich*? Follow the war cry: How to kill an adjective!

Avoid vague words like *walk, laugh, pour*. Be creative. The boy *ambled, shuffled, swaggered*; the villain *scoffed, jeered, sneered*; water *gurgled, gushed, spurted out*.

Avoid meaningless words like *thing, something, somewhere*. Be definite. Name the thing or place, use concrete words that evoke clear images.

Get a thesaurus to help you, of course use it with caution.

A dictionary of synonyms helps too.

Choose words that convey your message clearly to readers. Good writers look for the apt word, the word that carries the precise denotation and the strongest, richest connotations.

Creative Writing Tip #4: Be Concise

Concise writing is clear and strong. Write to the point, cut out unnecessary words. This doesn't mean that you throw out all details, descriptions and figures of speech but that you make every word pull its weight.

Cut out meaningless words and phrases like *basically, personally, as a matter of fact*.

As a matter of fact, today is my birthday has the same meaning as *Today is my birthday*.

Personally, I feel we shouldn't go near the bull: can anyone ever *feel* impersonally?

Don't repeat yourself. Phrases like *round in shape, the reason is because, revert back*, say the same thing twice.

Use strong action verbs. Sentences with active verbs are shorter and stronger than those with passive verbs.

Active Verb: *The man bit the dog.*

Passive Verb: *The dog was bitten by the man.*

Replace roundabout phrases like *in the event of, by virtue of the fact that, by the name of*, with single words that do the same job, like *if, because, named*.

Phrases like *there is, there was, it was* dilute your meaning:

There was a baby crying in the basket;
it was the baby's cry that woke him up.

Cut out the verbiage: *A baby was crying in the basket; the baby's cry woke him up.*

Connotation Denotation for Persuasive Writing

The synergy in "connotation denotation" interplays of words is necessary to improve writing skills by choosing apt words for every occasion.

Creative Writing Tip #1 on "Connotation Denotation" Synergy: Proper Word Choices

Effective writing depends on apt choice of words. To choose the right word for each context, you need to understand the "connotation denotation" synergy of words. Every word has a denotation, its explicit meaning. It also has connotations: the emotional overtones the word carries or (to put it another way) the emotions it evokes in readers.

Good writers strive to find the right words, the words that best fit their meaning and, at the same time, evoke strong emotions in readers.

Creative Writing Tip #2 on "Connotation Denotation" Synergy: Examples of Denotation According to Dictionary Definitions

The denotation of a word is its meaning or definition as listed in a dictionary. Using words according to their established denotations is important if you expect readers to grasp your meaning accurately.

Some words may seem to be interchangeable because they have the same general definitions, but in fact they are differentiated by subtle shades of meaning. Take, for example, the word *famous*; compare the different kinds and degrees of fame in the words *noted, well-known, distinguished, celebrated, talked-of, marked* and *notorious*.

Confusion may also arise because of similar-sounding words like *apposite* and *opposite*; *overlook* and *oversee*; *elusive* and *illusive*; *affect* and *effect*; or homonyms like *born* and *borne*; *discreet* and *discrete*; *stationary* and *stationery*.

Wrong choice of words distorts a writer's message, often with (unintended) hilarious results. Look up a good dictionary if you're unsure about the exact meaning of a word.

Creative Writing Tip #3 on "Connotation Denotation" Synergy: What is Denotation that Delights Readers?

Choose words that precisely fit your meaning. Words do not work in isolation; they complement one another. When all the words fit and flow together in a harmonious whole, the result is a delightful experience for the reader.

Creative Writing Tip #4 on "Connotation Denotation" Synergy: What is Connotation?

Some words also have connotations: ideas, associations and emotional overtones that go beyond the word's explicit definition. Such words pulsate with life, awakening emotions in readers.

Words with approximately similar meanings may have subtly or even entirely different connotations. For example, what images and feelings do the following phrases trigger in you: *lean, hungry look; haggard, starved look; gaunt, wolfish look*?

If you are unsure of the connotations of words, consult a good dictionary of synonyms.

Creative Writing Tip #5 on "Connotation Denotation" Synergy: Examples of Connotations that Enrich One Another

Sentences are especially potent when constructed with emotionally-charged words because of the rich interactions among their connotations; each word enriches the others, so that the whole is greater than the sum of its parts.

Explore the emotional overtones in different words, and the overall effect when putting the words together in sentences.

Creative Writing Tip #6 on "Connotation Denotation" Synergy: How Denotation and Connotation Affect Tone and Mood

Word choice determines tone and mood. The combinations and arrangements of words, together with the interplay of their emotional overtones, give a unique flavour to a piece of writing, a distinct tone and mood.

Figurative Language

Figurative language makes your writing come alive! You can use figures of speech such as metaphors, similes, personification, hyperboles, oxymoron, synecdoche and more, to improve your writing skills.

Creative Writing Tips on Use of Figurative Language

Examples of Metaphors

When we use a metaphor, we imply a comparison (indirectly, without using the word *as* or *like*) between an idea or quality and a concrete picture.

For example, the abstract idea of *lost years* comes alive when we pair it with an action picture: *the years the swarming locusts have eaten, the cankerworm, and the caterpillar.*

Metaphors can also create a mood
Her eyes are homes of silent prayer,
Nor other thought her mind admits...

Examples of Similes

A simile sharpens and enhances an idea through direct association or comparison with concrete images, using the word *as* or *like*. Examples:
I wandered lonely as a cloud
That floats on high o'er vales and hills...

Or
The Assyrian came down like the wolf on the fold,
And his cohorts were gleaming in purple and gold;
And the sheen of their spears was like stars on the sea...

Examples of Personification

Personification brings ideas and objects to life by treating them as though they were human. This is how one author has infused warmth and personality into commonplace fruit and vegetables:
Ruddy, brown-faced, broad-girthed Spanish Onions, shining in the fatness of their growth like Spanish Friars, and winking from their shelves in wanton slyness at the girls as they went by...

Examples of Irony

Irony spices up your writing; by implying the opposite of what is actually said, irony creates nuances that intrigue readers and add to their enjoyment. The effect can range from lighthearted humour to biting sarcasm or ridicule:
It is a truth universally acknowledged, that a single man in possession of a good fortune must be in want of a wife.

Examples of Hyperbole

This is an overstatement or deliberate exaggeration, used to create humour or emphasise a point:
Had we but world enough, and time,
This coyness, Lady, were no crime
We would sit down and think which way
To walk and pass our long love's day...

> *An hundred years should go to praise*
> *Thine eyes and on thy forehead gaze;*
> *Two hundred to adore each breast,*
> *But thirty thousand to the rest.*
> *An age at least to every part,*
> *And the last age should show your heart.*
> *For, Lady, you deserve this state,*
> *Nor would I love at lower rate.*
> (From *To His Coy Mistress*, by Andrew Marvell)

Examples of Understatement

An understatement, or litotes, is the opposite of a hyperbole. We use it for irony or emphasis.

Examples: *He was a little displeased* (meaning: he was furious); *How was the concert? Not bad at all* (meaning: it was very good).

Examples of Oxymora ("Oxymorons")

Here, we juxtapose two opposites for a seeming contradiction or paradox; nevertheless this contrast conveys precisely the meaning we intend, and the unexpected word combination grabs the reader's attention. Examples: *proud humility; cold hospitality; thunderous silence*.

An oxymoron can evoke fresh, vigorous images: for example, this description of goldfish in a bowl that *went gasping round and round their little world in slow and passionless excitement*.

Examples of Synecdoche

Here we use the specific to represent the general (or vice versa); or a part to represent the whole (or vice versa);

or a person to represent a class (or vice versa): useful for replacing vague or colourless words with vibrant images. For example, *sceptre and crown* to represent rulers; *scythe and spade* to represent peasants, as in:

Sceptre and Crown
Must tumble down,
And in the dust be equal made
With the poor crooked scythe and spade

Strong Action Verbs

One can grab the readers' attention with vivid verbs, powerful verbs. One must harness the tremendous power in action verbs:

Tips on Action Verbs

#1: Vivid Verbs Are Powerful Verbs

Verbs energise. An action verb generates more drama and emotion than a noun, adjective or adverb of similar meaning. Compare:

The children wept when their dog died. (Strong verbs: *wept, died*)

The children shed tears over the death of their dog. (Nouns: *tears, death*)

The children were sad when their dog was dead. (Weak verb *to be* + adjectives: *sad, dead*)

Use vivid verbs, powerful verbs, to fizz up the action, paint word-pictures, and evoke feelings in your readers.

#2: Active Verbs Grab Attention

Use active verbs rather than passive. Active verbs rivet readers' attention; passive verbs weaken your writing. Compare:

Tina broke the jar. (Active verb)

The jar was broken by Tina. (Passive verb)

The first example is strong, precise and concise; the second sounds insipid.

The active verb in the first example charges the sentence with a vitality and directness that compels attention. In the second example, however, the passive verb has slowed down the action and made the sentence unnecessarily wordy.

#3: Active Verbs Add Vim and Vitality

Active verbs get things done fast; passive verbs impede action. Compare:

India fired the rocket. (Active verb)

The rocket was fired by India. (Passive verb)

Use active verbs to quicken the pace. Like this:

...the carriage dashed through streets and swept round corners, with women screaming before it, and men clutching each other and clutching children out of its way.

#4: Concise Verbs Are Strong Verbs

Some forms of verbs are more concise, direct and dramatic than others. Compare:

The clock is striking twelve.

The clock strikes twelve.

Verbs ending in -*ing* (for example, *striking, prowling, shouting*) are weaker than their shorter forms (*strike, prowl, shout*).

#5: Powerful Verbs Are Concise and Precise

Be as concise as possible; prefer the single verb to the roundabout phrase.

Do not say:
He did not remember to feed the dog.
She did not pass the music exam.

Say instead:
He forgot to feed the dog.
She failed the music exam.

#6: Examples of Action Verbs

A strong verb creates a mood or an image simply by its sound or connotations: for example, instead of the word *walk*, use more evocative words like *saunter, stride, strut* or *swagger*. Water can *gush, gurgle, spurt* or *squirt out*; villains may *scoff, sneer, jeer* or *taunt*; and as for the loot, let it *gleam, glitter, sparkle* or *dazzle*.

Vivid verbs appeal to the reader's senses of sight, sound, touch or smell. Like these:
Falstaff sweats to death,
And lards the lean earth as he walks along.

#7: Strong Verbs & Verb Music

Strong verbs also evoke the music of words. When choosing verbs, discern with your inner ear: do the sounds of the words carry the meaning and mood you want to convey? Is it melody or discord that you hear? Do the verbs stimulate this word music for readers?

NOTE: When to Use Passive Verbs
When is it better to use passive verbs? When the story calls

for a change of pace: for example, to slow down the action, reduce tension, or stretch the narrative.

Choose passive verbs also when you want to emphasise the receiver of the action.

"Subject Verb Object" Variations

When every sentence structure falls into the same old "Subject Verb Object" mould, writing starts to sound monotonous. This needn't be the case; English syntax is flexible, and lets you play with sentence structure variations to create word music.

Positions of Emphasis

When you read a sentence, the parts most likely to catch your attention and stay in your mind are the beginning and end; we call them the positions of emphasis, with the stronger position at the close of the sentence.

Writers call attention to important ideas by putting them at the beginnings and ends of sentences. This makes it easier for readers to grasp the meaning and remember important points. It also gives sentences a rhythmic flow, as in these examples:

Mary had a little lamb.
Why didn't they ask Evans?
Ask and you shall receive.

Variations in Climactic Order

Another way of calling attention to key ideas is by placing them in climactic order: that is, arranging them in order of increasing importance or impact. This arrangement builds up suspense in a sentence.

What you choose to emphasise determines your sentence structure. Let's say you want to tell readers about your dog Ginger - a lovely golden retriever, if a little on the plump side (he does so love his food). You could highlight any of these points by leading up to it:

He's *gorgeous*:
This is my dog Ginger: he's a golden retriever, and you can see he's really beautiful.

He's *mine*:
This beautiful golden retriever with the slight waddle is my dog Ginger.

He does have a *problem*, though:
This is my dog Ginger: this greedy little golden retriever that's got to go on a diet.

Repetition Emphasises Key Elements

You can also emphasise important points by repeating key words or phrases. Repetition links related ideas and gives sentences a lyrical rhythm. For example:

*When I was **a child**, I spoke **as a child**, I understood **as a child**, I thought **as a child**; but when I became a man, I put away **child**ish things.*
(From *The Bible, 1 Corinthians 13:11*)

You can repeat pronouns, adjectives, verbs or conjunctions to emphasise key elements and create word music. Repetition also changes the sentence structure and gives it a "piling-on" effect:

***Thy** rod and **Thy** staff, they comfort me.*

or

*My love is like a **red, red** rose.*

Combine Repetition with Climactic Order

For powerful, lyrical language build your ideas up in climactic order, at the same time repeating key words or phrases:

*Love is patient, **love is** kind; **love does not** envy, **love does not** parade itself, **it is not** puffed up; **it is not** rude, **it is not** self-seeking; **is not** provoked; thinks no evil; **does not rejoice in** iniquity, but **rejoices in** the truth; bears **all things**, believes **all things**, hopes **all things**, endures **all things**. Love never fails.*
(From *The Bible, 1 Corinthians 13: 4-8*)

Inversions

If all your words seem to plod along at the same mundane pace, add an element of surprise by varying your sentence structures. One way of doing this is through inversion of word order.

Sentence structures in English usually follow an orderly sequence of subject-verb-object/complement. Any change in this arrangement, like putting the verb before the subject, or the object/complement before the subject, draws attention to itself. Such inversions are especially useful when you want to highlight key words.

A child is born to us, a son is given to us.

Sounds flat? How about these "in"-versions:

For unto us a child is born, unto us a son is given.

(From *The Bible, Isaiah 9:6*)

Hear the music, feel the excitement in these latter versions? That's the difference inversion makes.

Parallel Structure

Parallel structure, or parallelism, is a special kind of repetition that relies on the balance between related words or phrases to create word music.

You can construct parallel structures by pairing related words or phrases. This balance gives sentences a rhythmic flow and coherence - especially so, where the parallel pairs contain repetitions of the same word or phrase:

It was the best of times, it was the worst of times, it was the age of wisdom, it was the age of foolishness, it was the epoch of belief, it was the epoch of incredulity, it was the season of Light, it was the season of Darkness, it was the spring of hope, it was the winter of despair, we had everything before us, we had nothing before us, we were all going direct to Heaven, we were all going direct the other way...

(From *A Tale of Two Cities* by Charles Dickens)

Note the repetition of *it was*, *we had* and *we were*, and the balanced pairs: *the best of times/the worst of times; the age of wisdom/the age of foolishness; the spring of hope/the winter of despair...*

Use the rhythm of parallel structures to help you deliver a powerful message to your readers.

Parallel Structure and Ellipses

You can omit words if the meaning remains clear without them; such contractions, known as ellipses, can result in more concise, powerful writing. Ellipses are especially effective in parallel structures, and often give a better balance to sentences:

Homer was the greater genius, Virgil the better artist. In one we most admire the man, in the other the work... Homer, like the Nile, pours out his riches with a boundless overflow; Virgil, like a river in its banks, with a gentle and constant stream.
(From *Preface to The Illiad of Homer*, by Alexander Pope)

Where there is hatred, let me sow love;
Where there is injury, pardon;
Where there is doubt, faith;
Where there is despair, hope;
Where there is darkness, light;
And where there is sadness, joy.
(From *Prayer of St Francis of Assisi*)

Parallel Structure and Climactic Order

Use parallel structures to emphasise key points; present your ideas in a series of balanced words or phrases arranged in climactic order - that is, in order of increasing importance or dramatic impact. Parallel structures in climactic order create the most forceful impression upon readers; as in these examples:

It is a far, far better thing that I do, than I have ever done; it is a far, far better rest that I go to, than I have ever known.
(From *A Tale of Two Cities* by Charles Dickens)

Short Story Writing: TIPS

1. **Have a clear theme**	What is the story about? That doesn't mean what is the plot line, the sequence of events or the character's actions; it means what is the underlying message or statement behind the words. Get this right and your story will have more resonance in the minds of your readers.
2. **An effective short story covers a very short time span**	It may be one single event that proves pivotal in the life of the character, and that event will illustrate the theme.
3. **Don't have too many characters**	Each new character will bring a new dimension to the story, and for an effective short story too many diverse dimensions will dilute the theme. Have only enough characters to effectively illustrate the theme. There is only one leit-motif in a short story.
4. **Make every word count**	There is no room for unnecessary expansion in a short story. If each word is not working towards putting across the theme, delete it.
5. **Focus**	The best stories are the ones that follow a narrow subject line. What is the point of your story? Its point is its theme. It's tempting to digress, but in a 'short' you have to follow the straight and narrow otherwise you end up with either a novel beginning or a hodgepodge of ideas that add up to nothing.

Structure of Your Short Story

How to structure your short stories:
- Put a man up a tree
- Throw stones at him
- Get him down

When you come to think of it, it's good advice for any writer. So follow the steps in the plan below to start writing great short stories.

Short Story Plan

Start with a situation - a problem to be resolved for your protagonist (the man up the tree).

Then present the problems that can occur (throw some stones):
- Misunderstandings/mistaken identity/lost opportunities etc

The final step is to show how you can solve the problem - get the man down from his leafy perch - safely.
- Love triumphs/good conquers evil/honesty is the best policy/united we stand

Short Story Theme

Every piece of writing must have a message or thread of meaning running through it, and this theme is the skeleton or framework on which you hang your plot, characters, setting etc.

As you write, make sure that every word is related to this theme.

It's tempting to use your short story to show off your talents at characterisation, descriptive writing, dialogue or whatever ... But every excess word is a word that dilutes the impact of your story.

The best stories are the ones that follow a narrow subject line. Decide what the point of your story is and even though it's tempting to digress, you must stick to the point otherwise you end up with either a novel beginning or a mish-mash of ideas that add up to nothing.

Time Span for Your Short Story

An effective short story covers a very short time span. It may be one single event that is momentous in the life of your main character or the story may take place in a single day or even an hour. Try to use the events you depict to illustrate your theme.

Setting for Your Short Story

Because you have such a limited number of words to convey your message, you must choose your settings carefully ... there's no room for free-loaders in a short story!

That doesn't mean you have to be trite or predictable when deciding on settings. For example, some of the most frightening settings for thrillers are not cemeteries or lonely alleys, but normal places where readers can imagine themselves.

Appeal to your readers' five senses to make your settings more real.

Characters in Your Short Story

Around three main characters is all a short story can effectively deal with because too many will distract you from your theme.

Don't give in to the urge to provide detailed background on your characters ... decide on the characteristics that are important for your theme and stick to those. If you fall in love with your character, use him/her as the basis for a novel later on.

Mix and match characteristics to come up with memorable characters for all your stories.

Short Story Dialogue

Never underestimate the power of dialogue in conveying character, but it must contribute to the main focus of the story - don't just use it to pad out your characters. Every word you put into the mouth of your characters must contribute to revealing your theme ... if it doesn't, be ruthless and cut it.

Vivid Imagery for Your Short Story

Vivid imagery also draws the reader in.

Capture the reader's interest in, and empathy for, your characters. You need to paint such a vivid picture that the reader can imagine himself or herself to be in the scene. Again this goes back to placing yourself there and transposing this into your writing as we discussed earlier. That involvement is often referred to as reader empathy. And an empathetic reader lives the fictional dream.

Plot for Your Short Story

Begin with an arresting first paragraph or lead, enough to grab the readers and make them curious to know what happens next.

Make sure your plot works - there must be a beginning,

a middle and an end. But don't spend too much time on the build-up, so that the climax or denouement (as in the twist ending) is relegated to one sentence. And don't signal the twist ending too soon - try to keep the reader guessing until the last moment.

If you're telling a fast-moving story, say crime, then keep your paragraphs and sentences short. It's a trick that sets the pace and adds to the atmosphere you're conveying to the reader.

How to Write (and Finish) a Novel

According to Kurt Vonnegut, "The primary benefit of practicing any art, whether well or badly, is that it enables one's soul to grow." If this is true, then nothing makes for more mature souls than writing a novel, a form that particularly requires perseverance and patience. Though there are no hard and fast rules for how to get from first draft to bookstore shelf, these guideposts will help you find your way.

1. Give Some Thought to Plot

Writing a novel can be a messy undertaking. The editing process will go easier if you devote time to the plot in the beginning. For some writers, this means an outline; others work with index cards, putting a different scene on each one. Still others only have a conflict and a general idea of where they plan to end up before diving in. If you're just starting out, then this may be something you'll learn about your writing process as you revise your first novel.

2. Get a First Draft Down

Though it is a good idea to test your idea out on other writers, resist getting feedback on the writing itself at this stage. Focus on getting the complete story down on paper instead. You may have trouble with writer's block or tend to let projects stall.

3. Be Prepared to Revise

One must be prepared for the amount of work between first draft and published book. However inspired you might feel while writing it, the first draft will probably be bad. It will be clunky, disorganised, and confusing. Entire chapters will drag. The dialogue will be unconvincing and stiff. This is the way for everyone. And like writers everywhere, you just have to roll up your sleeves and get to work rewriting it.

4. Solicit Feedback

When you think it's time to start contacting agents, get feedback from writers you trust. Don't be surprised if they send you back to your desk for another draft. Address any large structural problems first, and then go through the book scene by scene. Anytime you have a question about whether something is working, stop and see what you could do to make it better. If you want your book to be good, revise with your most intelligent, most thoughtful reader in mind.

5. Put It Aside

If you find yourself coming up against the same problems with every draft, it may be time to work on something else for awhile. Sixteen years elapsed between the first draft of Jane Austen's *Pride and Prejudice* and the published version, for instance. If you find yourself losing your way, go back to the fun parts of writing. Create something new; read for fun. With each new project you take on and each book you read, you'll learn new lessons. When you come back to the novel — and you will come back — you'll see it with more experienced eyes.

Conflict and Character within Story Structure

The Basic Three Act Structure

The simplest building blocks of a good story are found in the Three Act Structure. Separated by Plot Points, its Act 1 (Beginning), Act 2 (Middle), and Act 3 (End) refer not to where in time in the story they lie but instead fundamental stages along the way.

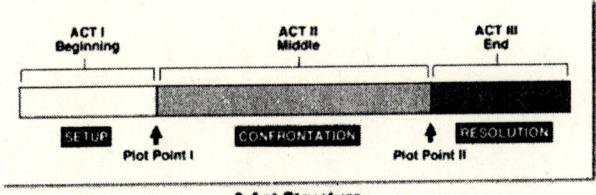

3 Act Structure

In the Beginning you introduce the reader to the setting, the characters and the situation (conflict) they find themselves in and their goal. Plot Point 1 is a situation that drives the main character from their "normal" life toward some different conflicting situation that the story is about. Great stories often begin at Plot Point 1, thrusting the main character right into the thick of things, but they never really leave out Act 1, instead filling it in with back story along the way.

In the Middle the story develops through a series of complications and obstacles, each leading to a mini crisis. Though each of these crises are temporarily resolved, the story leads inevitably to an ultimate crisis—the Climax. As the story progresses, there is a rising and falling of tension with each crisis, but an overall rising tension as we approach the Climax. The resolution of the Climax is Plot Point 2.

In the End, the Climax and the loose ends of the story are resolved during the Denouement. Tension rapidly dissipates because it's nearly impossible to sustain a reader's interest very long after the climax. Finish your story and get out.

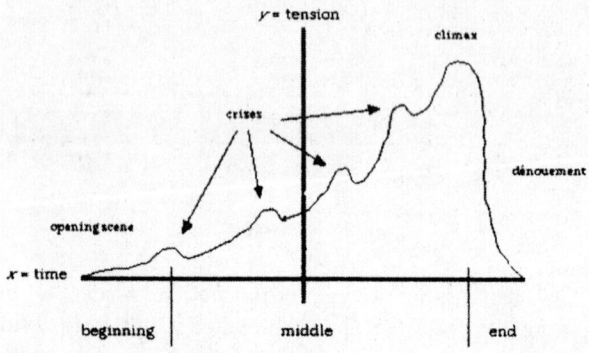

Character Arc and Story Structure

Act 1

- In the Beginning of a story the main character, being human (even if he of she isn't), will resist change (inner conflict). The character is perfectly content as he is; there's no reason to change.

Plot Point 1 – Then something happens to throw everything off balance.

- It should come as a surprise that shifts the story in a new direction and reveals that the protagonist's life will never be the same again.
- It puts an obstacle in the way of the character that forces him or her to deal with something they would avoid under normal circumstances.

Act 2

- The second Act is about a character's emotional journey and is the hardest part of a story to write. Give your characters all sorts of challenges to overcome during Act 2. Make them struggle towards their goal.
- **The key to Act Two is *conflict*.** Without it you can't move the story forward. And conflict doesn't mean a literal fight. Come up with obstacles (maybe five, maybe a dozen—depends on the story) leading up to your plot point at the end of Act 2.
- Throughout the second act remember to ***continually raise the stakes*** of your character's emotional journey.
- Simultaneously advance both inner and outer conflicts. Have them work together—the character should

alternate up and down internally between hope and disappointment as external problems begin to seem solvable then become more insurmountable than ever.
- Include reversals of fortune and unexpected turns of events—surprise your reader with both the actions of the main character and the events surrounding him.

Plot Point 2
- Act Two ends with the second plot point, which thrusts the story in another unexpected direction.
- Plot Point 2 occurs at the moment the hero appears beaten or lost but something happens to turn the situation around. The hero's goal becomes reachable.
  - Right before this unexpected story turn, the hero reaches *the Black Moment*—the point at which all is lost and the goal cannot be achieved.
    - In order to have a "Climax", where the tension is highest, you must have a "Black" moment, where the stakes are highest and danger at its worst.
    - During this moment, the hero draws upon the new strengths or lessons he's learned in order to take action and bring the story to a conclusion.

Act 3

- The third Act dramatically shows how the character is able to succeed or become a better person.
- Resolution/denouement ties together the loose ends of the story (not necessarily all of them) and allows the reader to see the outcome of the main character's decision at the climax. Here we see evidence of the change in a positive character arc.

Story Structure

Great novels—great stories—existed long before there were books about something called Story Structure. The story has 3 essential elements: Plot, Character and Moral intent. Of course in literary terms there is a subtle difference between 'story' and 'plot': story is 'life in time'; plot is 'life in values'.

NOTE: Plot

Don't let your focus be the Plot, which is the series of events and situations that occur along the route of your story. The Plot is a natural outcome of the seeds of your story—it *emerges* from your setup of the characters, their conflicts and the setting they occur in. You'll write a more powerful, believable story if you focus on seed planting long before you worry about the harvest.

Tips for Writing Poetry

'A Poem must not mean. But Be'
Writing poetry can frustrate or reward beyond words.

A Few Poetry-writing Tips

- **First, read examples of and learn about the poetic form you wish to write.** There is no single poem writing rule. Many want to know how to write a love poem, lyric poetry, a poem about writing, a haiku poem, a narrative poem. Each has its own writing style. Some poetry is written in forms, each form having its own rules. Some poetry is free verse, or '*vers libre*' which either creates its own set of unique rules for that poem or has no rules. Concrete poems draw pictures with the words as they are arranged on a page. So, read poems and learn from them what you'd like to write.

- **Use excited and exciting language.** Pay attention to sound, rhythm, thought. Disrupt the obvious. It is true 'Poetry language is so excited, it becomes multiple of meaning.' But remember: Poetry is appreciated before it is understood.
- **Focus on small, specific observations** and avoid broad, general topics (such as "love," "war," or "religion"). Let the broad, general themes emerge from the specific and detailed observances of everyday life and events.
- **Use sensory details**—sound, sight, smell, touch, taste—and be specific. Like Shelley you may develop the oddity of synesthethic imagery.
- **Explore new possibilities**, and don't use clichés and other tired phrases. Ezra Pound said, "Make it new."
- **Keep a journal** where you can jot down words, thoughts, images as they occur to you. Gather them later into a "found" poem of your own words.
- **Reading and writing poetry can be very fulfilling activities by themselves.** The best poetry writing tip, though, is to read poetry in order to write a good poem. Read the type of poetry you want to write: love poem, narrative poem, Valentine poem, Haiku poem, lyric poem, or a concrete poem.
- **Use your journal to write about the reading you do.** Don't just respond to the content, but notice how the poem is written, how it looks on the page, how it sounds read out loud. Respond by writing a similar poem to one you love or a better poem than one you hate. Use the journal for reading and writing.

10 More Tips for Writing Poetry

1. Pay attention to the world around you—little things, big things, people, animals, buildings, events, etc. What do you see, hear, taste, smell, feel?
2. Listen to words and sentences. What kind of music do they have? How is the music of poetry different from the music of songs?
3. Read all kinds of poetry. Which poems do you like and why?
4. Read what you write out loud. How does it sound? How could it sound better?
5. Ask yourself: does this poem have to rhyme? Would it be good or better if it didn't? If it should rhyme, what kind of rhyme would be best? (For example, 1st and 2nd lines rhyme; 3rd and 4th lines rhyme—"Roses are red/So is your head/Violets are blue/So is your shoe"; or 1st and 3rd lines rhyme; 2nd and 4th lines rhyme—"What is your name?/Who is your mother?/This poem is quite lame/I should try another."
6. Ask yourself: does this poem sound phoney? Don't stick in big words or extra words just because you think a poem ought to have them.
7. A title is part of a poem. It can tell you what the poem is about. It can even be another line of the poem. Keats in *Ode on a Grecian Urn* addresses the Urn itself: "Thou still unravished bride of quietness".
8. Before you write, think about what you want your whole poem to say.
9. If you end up saying something else, that's okay, too.
10. Go wild. Be funny. Be serious. Be whatever you want! Use your imagination, your own way of seeing.

Writing in the Workplace

10 Golden Rules

1. Start – attitude to create confidence and warm feeling about your company.
2. Keep in mind – you are selling – think as a salesman.
3. To influence people – to talk in the readers language.
4. To talk his language – stop answering letters and start answering people.
5. Be a letter detective to answer people.
6. Form the habit of studying every inquiry for clues to the written nature and personality.
7. Transport – form a picture of the writer.
8. Write as your friend.
9. While answering Formal letters, dig. Little deeper – his basic interest.
10. Lack of knowledge of your business takes extra pain to make your answer full of understanding.

Five Business Writing Tips

Tip #1

It helps to imagine a conversation with your reader. For example, if you are writing to announce a meeting, imagine telling someone face-to-face about the meeting. That person would ask:

- Why are we meeting?
- When is it?
- Where?

- What's the agenda?
- Who will be there?
- Do I have to attend? What if I can't?
- Do I need to prepare? How?

List all the questions your reader may have. Then consider the order in which your reader would ask them. If you have listed any of the questions in a different order, re-arrange them to meet your reader's needs.

Now, one by one, write the answers to your reader's questions. For example:
- Why are we meeting?
  We are meeting to decide whether...
- When is it?
  The meeting takes place on Monday, April 27, at 2 p.m. for no more than 45 minutes.

Go through each one of your reader's questions and answer it. When you're finished, you're not only finished organising—you're finished writing! Just edit, proofread, and send.

Business Writing Tip #2

Be Positive!

State what *to* do—not what to avoid.
  Yes: Always process orders within two days.
  No: Never take more than two days to process an order.

Say what you *can* do—not what you can't do.
  Yes: We can meet first thing Monday morning.
  No: We can't meet now. It has to wait until Monday morning.

Use neutral rather than blaming language.
   Yes: Let me clarify what I meant.
   No: You misunderstood what I said.

Use words that create a positive feeling.
   Yes: At this company we value natural resources.
   No: At this company we don't waste natural resources.

Take every opportunity to communicate positively.
   Yes: Thank you for your letter.
   No: We have received your letter.

Don't be negative! **Be positive.**

Tip #3

Know Where Passive Verbs Belong

Be careful of a fault called "Passive Voice. Rewrite with an active voice verb."

"Your gift *is appreciated*" (passive) to "We *appreciate* your gift" (active). This is another fine suggestion. "Is appreciated" sounds impersonal, whereas "We appreciate" feels warm.

When we make these changes, we are replacing wordy, vague phrases with concise, direct words. That's excellent.

But there are places where passive verbs fit just right:
1. When you don't know who performed the action.
   Passive: Her car *was stolen* twice.
   Not: Someone stole her car twice.
2. When it doesn't matter who performs the action.
   Passive: The logs *are pre-cut*.
   Not: A worker pre-cuts the logs.
3. When we want to avoid blaming someone.

Passive: The books *were lost.*
Not: Derek lost the books.
4. When we want to soften a directive.
Passive: This paragraph *could be shortened.*
Not: Shorten this paragraph.

Tip #4 More With Less!

For over a decade, the message at work has been "Do more with less!"

We can be much *more* efficient if we use *less* wordiness. By cutting down on extra words, we cut down on both writing and reading time.

The paragraph below contains 70 words.

This document is for the purpose of giving the reader a detailed explanation of the inventory process. It describes the activities we currently do in the majority of instances on a daily and weekly basis. In order to provide an introduction to the process for employees who work on a temporary basis, we also have prepared an overview, which describes the highlights of the inventory process in just two pages.

Here is a 30-word revision:

This document explains the inventory process in detail. It describes our usual daily and weekly activities. We also have prepared a two-page overview to introduce the process to temporary employees.

To lighten up your sentences, watch for heavy phrases like these:

for the purpose of = for
the majority of = most

in order to	=	to
provide an introduction	=	introduce
on a daily basis	=	daily
on a regular basis	=	routinely

It's true—we *can* do more with less!

TIP #5

Every now and then we get stuck. The blank screen or empty page just stares at us dully. Meanwhile, the digital clock shifts through the minutes. We fidget.

Need to break through writer's block? Then do it—break out of what you are doing and try something different. Here are a few techniques.

Imagine that you are talking with your reader. Think about the things your reader wants or needs to hear. Then "tell" (write) any part—beginning, middle, or end. Don't worry about the perfect opening.

Write without censoring yourself. Pay no attention to whether the writing is good. Just let the words and ideas flow. Then choose your "keepers" and build from them.

Review some of your past writing that makes you feel proud. This look will build your confidence and may give you specific ideas.

Talk with co-workers. Don't wait until you're done to tell about your struggles. The screen is blank *now*.

For a project that takes several sittings, end a sitting when you know what comes next, and make a note of it. That way, you won't face a mental block when you begin the next time.

Take a break that includes a change of scenery, or shift to another activity.

When you're stuck near the end of a piece and have covered everything, quit.

Business Letters

Virtue
Make your letters *pleasant*. A good business letter has these initial virtues.

Prompt
Always reply at once. Delay often means muddle,

Literate
Show that you have mastered the essentials of accidence, syntax, punctuation etc. Make a rough draft first.

Easy to read
Pay attention to spacing; make good margins and reasonably short paragraphs.

Accurate
Pay scrupulous attention to all details of time, place, and quantity etc. Get addresses and dates right. Don't over-abbreviate.

Short and straight forward
Keep your sentences short and *to the point*. Don't ramble. Conciseness is essential.

Appropriate
Bear in mind who your correspondent is. Adjust each letter to the needs of the recipient. It is better to be a foot too formal than an inch too familiar.

Natural

Be sincere and unaffected by official jargon. Avoid exaggerated flattery or servility in letters to superiors.

Tactful

Always be willing to admit a mistake. Cultivate politeness and courtesy, and avoid sarcasm and rudeness. Even when the necessity arises for writing a "strong" letter remember that the iron hand is just as effective in the velvet glove.

Guidelines

1. Before you begin writing a business letter, define clearly your purpose in writing. Make sure that you have a clear idea of:
   - the events that have led to your writing the letter
   - your maximum aims (the most you can hope to achieve)
   - your realistic aims (what you expect to achieve)
   - the information you need to explain in the letter
   - the arguments you need to deploy
2. The **first paragraph** of the letter should introduce the subject matter and either state or imply your purpose in writing.
3. The **body** of the letter should consist of one or more paragraphs. It should develop clearly and logically the argument and facts of the case. If there is more than one paragraph, each paragraph should focus on a separate aspect of the subject matter and there should be clear links between the paragraphs.
4. The **final paragraph** should leave the reader in no doubt about your attitude towards the subject of the letter. It may, for example, spell out what you

would like to see happen. It should be positive and unambiguous.
5. Although the reader of your letter may be unknown to you, it is important to achieve a suitable **tone** in your writing. So, as far as possible, **avoid:**
   - jargon
   - too many long sentences
   - using the passive
   - letting your feelings get the better of you
   - trying to be too clever
   - being too blunt
6. Adopt a letter layout that is clear and consistent.
7. If you are writing to someone whose name and title you do not know, use the greeting Dear Sir or Madam, and the ending 'yours faithfully', signing yourself with your initials and surname.
8. If you are writing to a named person, address them as Dear Mr/Mrs/Miss/Ms-, and end 'yours sincerely', followed by your first name and surname.
9. If you have met them or spoken to them by phone, or otherwise feel that you have some acquaintance with them, address them by their first name and sign yourself 'yours sincerely', using your first name.

Business Writing Skills

Make a writing plan
This helps you stay focused and relevant and ultimately, saves you time writing.

Say why you are writing in the first sentence
Help your reader understand why you are writing by starting with an objective sentence. **Keep it short and**

sweet. Don't make your reader have to wade through long, rambling sentences. Avoid falling into the trap of using over-formal words such as "hereby" and "herewith". They will make you sound old-fashioned and pompous and don't add any meaning to your sentence. **Link your ideas**. Guide your reader through your text by using linking words and phrases. Words such as "and", "because" or "however" make your text flow and prevent your sentences from appearing isolated from each other.

Get the tone right
The tone of your text is the "voice" that you use with your reader, and the one you choose depends on who you are writing to, and why you are writing.

Keep your style appropriate and consistent
Bear in mind the formality of the situation.

End your correspondence by referring back to the reader
Make sure your reader knows what the next step should be. If you are asking for help in an email, you could end "Thanks for your help". In a letter you could write "I look forward to hearing from you."

Make sure your salutation and ending are correct
If you start a letter with "Dear Mr X" or "Dear Ms X", end "Yours sincerely" (or in American English, "Sincerely yours"). If you know your reader quite well, you can start "Dear + first name" and end with "Best wishes" or "Best/Kind regards". If you don't know the name of the person you are writing to and start "Dear Sir or Madam", end with "Yours faithfully" rather than "Yours sincerely".

You can also start and end emails in the same way as letters. But if you are writing to more than one person, you can omit the salutation completely and start with your objective. Other ways you can end emails is by writing "Thanks" or even "Cheers", but never "Bye".

Pay attention to your punctuation
Most common punctuation mistakes are made with capital letters, commas and apostrophes. Remember that commas are used in lists, and to separate clauses, to give a kind of "breathing space". Capital letters should be used for proper nouns, and in the first sentence of your correspondence. Apostrophes are used to show possession or contraction, but never for plurals.

Edit your writing
Read through what you have written to check for spelling and grammar mistakes.

Writing Minutes of a Meeting

Role of Minutes

- keep people informed of progress
- remind people *what* they should do and by *when*
- be a legal record of decisions

Type of Minutes

If you know why you're writing minutes, you can then decide what type of minutes you should produce.

Some options:
- a full verbatim record of what everyone said
- a full outline of the discussion plus any decisions and action points

- a brief outline of what was discussed plus decisions and action points
- only decisions and action points
- only decisions
- only action points.

Language for Writing Minutes

Write minutes in the past tense. You are writing about discussions that have already happened. When you are typing up the minutes from your notes, you are recording a past event.

Sethi **stated** that staff **needed** new uniforms. (correct)

Sethi **states** that staff **need** new uniforms. (incorrect)

Note that you have some choices as well.

You can write in the active voice:

Sujit expressed concern about customer service standards. (You are specifically identifying one person and what they said.)

Or you can use the passive voice:

Concern was expressed about customer service standards. (You are deliberately not saying who expressed concern.)

Preparing for the meeting

To prepare for the meeting, follow some steps:
- Get a copy of the agenda.
- Find out the meaning of terminology you don't understand.
- Read documents that will be tabled at the meeting.

Minute Notes Tips

- Have a template for writing notes. You could use columns: 'speaker', 'item', 'action'.

- Leave gaps to return to, if necessary.
- Interrupt if you didn't catch everything.
- Be prepared to review and summarise.

Tips for Writing Minutes

- Turn the notes into minutes while still fresh.
- Be accurate, brief and clear.
- Follow the order of the agenda.
- Highlight actions required.

HOW TO WRITE A MEMO

Memo (short for memorandum) is a business-oriented style that is best suited for inter-office or inter-colleague correspondence. More informal in tone and organisation than a letter, memos are generally used to provide or ask for information, announce a new policy, update on personnel transfers, or for any other internal issues.

Elements of an Effective Memo

An effective memo:
- grabs the reader's attention
- provides information, makes a recommendation, or asks for action
- supports your position or explains benefits to the reader
- mentions next steps and deadlines

Always take the four-step approach to writing: **plan** what you want to say, **write** a draft, **revise** the draft, and **edit**.

Types of Memos

There are four types of memos you might have to write, each with its own organisational format: information, problem-solving, persuasion, and internal memo proposal.

Information Memo

- used to deliver or request information or assistance
- first paragraph provides main idea
- second paragraph expands on the details
- third paragraph outlines the action required

Problem-solving Memo

- suggests a specific action to improve a situation
- first paragraph states the problem
- second paragraph analyses the problem
- third paragraph makes a recommendation
- when making a recommendation, include not only the positive details but also the drawbacks and diffuse them yourself

Persuasion Memo

- used to encourage the reader to undertake an action he or she doesn't have to take
- first paragraph begins with an agreeable point
- second paragraph introduces the idea
- third paragraph states benefits to the reader
- fourth paragraph outlines the action required
- fifth paragraph ends with a call to action

Internal Memo Proposal

- used to convey suggestions to senior management

- first paragraph states reason for writing
- second paragraph outlines present situation and states writer's proposal
- third paragraph describes advantage(s)
- fourth paragraph mentions and diffuses disadvantage(s)
- fifth paragraph ends with a call to action

Memo Parts

More informal in appearance and tone than a letter, a memo is set up in a special format. Headings, lists, tables or graphs are often used to make the information more readable.

All memos consist of two sections: the heading and the body. The heading indicates who is writing to whom, when, and why. The heading should include the following parts:

1. **To**
   - lists the names of everyone who will receive the memo
   - includes the first and last name and titles or departments of the recipients for formal memos, memos to superiors, or if everyone on the list does not know each other
   - if all recipients know each other's names and positions, use just the first initial and last name of each recipient
   - can be listed alphabetically or by rank
   - if it is not possible to fit all the names in the *To:* area, use the phrase "See distribution list"
   - at the end of the memo add the word "Distribution" and then list the names of the people who will receive a copy of the memo
   - arrange the names by rank, department or alphabetically

2. **From**
   - lists the name of the writer(s) in the same way as the name(s) of the recipient(s)
   - there is no complimentary close or signature line, but authors initial their names on the *From:* line
3. **Date**
   - lists the month, date, and year the memo was written
   - do not use abbreviations
   - avoid using numbers for months and days
4. **Re: or Subject**
   - indicates the main subject of the letter
   - should be as specific and concise as possible
5. **Cc or c**
   - lists those readers who should have a copy of the memo for their information or reference but are not expected to carry out the same action as the recipients listed in the *To:* line
   - "cc" can also be placed at the end of the memo below the distribution list (if used)

The body of the memo conveys the message and generally consists of 4 parts:

1. Introduction
   - states the general problem or main idea
2. Statement of facts
   - states the facts or discusses the problem or issue
3. Argument
   - explains importance or relevance of facts
4. Conclusion
   - summarises the main idea, suggests or requests action
   - memos do not have a complimentary close or signature line
   - memos end with a call to action

Email Writing

Email is a medium which has revolutionised the way in which we communicate with each other. In particular it is important to consider:

1. Why you are using email.
2. The ways in which emails differ from letters and telephone conversations these affect on:
   - how the email is 'topped and tailed'
   - the structure of the email
   - how attachments are used
   - how the email is formatted
3. How to use emails as effectively as possible. This involves:
   - Perspective
   - Reflection
   - Response
   - Organisation
4. Email etiquette:
   - formality
   - formatting
   - flaming
   - emoticons
   - initialises

Email Basics

The advent of email has revolutionised business and personal communication.

Emails inhabit a space somewhere between personal meetings, telephones, and letters. They share advantages with each of these means of communication. Like face-to-face meetings they are instant and direct and allow a number of people to participate. Like telephone calls they are quick and inexpensive. Like letters they allow those involved to keep a permanent record or messages sent and received. But once sent you cannot monitor the recipient's reaction to your message and then modify your message; when you receive them you may misjudge the sender's tone, because you only have words on the screen to go by. One of the advantages of emails is that they are quick to send. On the other hand, as in a face-to-face or telephone conversation, it is easy to say something that we soon regret. By contrast, letters take longer to compose and seem to allow more time for reflection before sending.

These elements matter
- Topping and tailing
- Structure
- Attachments
- Formatting

Topping and Tailing

When you compose an email you have to consider the frame within which your message is set. This consists of a number of elements:

Structure

As we've seen, an email can vary in length from one word to thousands. Short emails are often relaxed, informal, and unstructured. But longer messages usually need a clear structure.

Attachments

If your message is rather longer than this, you may prefer

to write it as a separate document and attach it to a covering email. Attaching separate documents has a number of advantages.

Formatting Emails

Email usually works in plain text mode. This means that you cannot use formatting features such as bold and italic text, or different fonts and font sizes.

Email Etiquette: Netiquette

Email does encourage a more relaxed way of writing than other more traditional forms of communication. Nevertheless a number of conventions have been established, which are often referred to as email etiquette.

1. Salutation and Formality

Like any form of communication, the salutation depends on the way you see your relationship with the other person.

2. Formatting

Even in plain text email it is possible to indicate emphasis. The most obvious way is to WRITE IN CAPITAL LETTERS. This is like raising your voice-it should only be used very sparingly, otherwise it just becomes irritating. Another way of emphasising a word or phrases is to put it between inverted commas: "This is very disappointing". Titles of books, films, etc. can be indicated by an underline.

3. Emotions

It is easy to respond over-emotionally to an email. This

phenomenon is sometimes referred to as '**flaming**'. It can be avoided in the ways already suggested: taking time to reflect, not sending messages off straightaway, and so on. You should also do everything you can to avoid your message being at all ambiguous. Jokes and irony can be very tricky when composing an email message.

Another method that some people use when corresponding with people they know well is to use emoticons: combinations of punctuation and letters that draw sideways faces.

Some people like using these, others hate them. Never use them in formal emails, though.

Emotion	Interpretation
:-)	Smiley face: can be used to express happiness or indicate a joke
:-(	Sad face
;-)	Wink: can be used to express irony/sarcasm
:-]	Very smiley face
:-c	Very unhappy
:-X	My lips are sealed
:-Q	I don't understand
:-P	Sticking one's tongue out
:'-(	Crying
:-/	Sceptical
:-o	Surprised
:-*	Kiss
O:-)	Angel
:-Y	Aside comment

:-[	Very sad face
:-I	Indifferent face
:-D	Surprise/shock/laughing
:-@	Scream
:-O	Shout/yell

4. Your Message in Its Context

a. Don't break the thread
When replying to a message do so by unsung 'Reply; rather than creating new message; this means that the thread of messages on a single subject can be kept together by those involved.

b. Reply to whom?
In general it is better not to 'Reply to all' unless there is a good reason for doing so. Work groups often set up their own rules on this.

c. Reply when?
Emails are a rapid form of communication. But they can go astray, and the sender is never entirely sure if they have arrived. For all these reasons it is helpful to reply promptly, even if only with a one-liner acknowledging receipt, and promising to answer more fully later.

d. Quoting in the reply
Another thing that bulks out emails unnecessarily is the habit of copying the whole of the message you have received in your reply. Some email clients do this by default, but it is usually possible to organise things so that the program copies only those parts that you want it to. Doing this can be very useful, especially if you have been asked a number of questions that you can follow each copied question with your answer.

e. Cc or Bcc?

Any email address you put in the 'Cc' slot can be read by anyone to whom you send the email. If you are sending a round robin message to a number of people who do not need to know each other's contact details, then you should put their email addresses in the 'Bcc' slot.

f. Forwarding

You may wish to forward a message you have received to someone else to whom it was not originally sent. There are a couple of things to remember here. The sender may not have wished anyone else but you to see the message at this stage, so it is only courteous to ask permission before forwarding it. Strictly speaking all messages are the copyright of the person who sent the mail so copying them without permission is a breach of the copyright law. In fact forwarding emails is normal practice within organisations or amongst other groups where there is a clear common goal and forwarding is expected by those concerned.

15 Tips for Composing Clear, Concise and Responsive Emails

1. Determine Your Desired Outcome
2. Quickly Answer, "What's the Point?"
3. State Benefits Clearly
4. Remember to KISS: *Keep it simple, stupid*
5. Save the Whole Story – Stick to the Facts
6. Pretend Face-to-face Intro
7. Text Message Trick
8. Avoid Excessive Compliments
9. Be Personal and Personable

email again so that you are sure you are not reading anything into the email that simply isn't there.
- If sending attachments, did you ask first when would be the best time to send? Did you check file size to make sure you don't fill the other side's inbox causing all subsequent e-mail to bounce?
- Refrain from using the Reply to all features to give your opinion to those who may not be interested. In most cases replying to the Sender alone is your best course of action.
- Make one last check that the address or addresses in the To: field are those you wish to send your reply to.
- Be sure your name is reflected properly.
- Type in complete sentences. To type random phrases or cryptic thoughts does not lend to clear communication.
- Never assume the intent of an email. If you are not sure – ask so as to avoid unnecessary misunderstandings.
- Just because someone doesn't ask for a response doesn't mean you ignore them. Always acknowledge emails from those you know in a timely manner.
- Be sure the Subject field accurately reflects the content of your email.
- Don't hesitate to say thank you, how are you, or appreciate your help!
- Keep emails brief and to the point. Save long conversations for the old fashioned telephone.
- Always end your emails with "Thank you," "Sincerely," "Take it easy," "Best regards" - something!

Formatting Emails

Do not type in all caps. That's yelling or reflects shouting: SCREAM it is called in Internet jargon.

10. Make it Easy to Be Found
11. Use Simple English
12. Font Matters
13. Formatting Matters
14. Minimise Questions
15. Trimming of Words

Netiquette Tips

- Make sure your e-mail includes a courteous greeting and closing. Helps to make your e-mail not seem demanding or terse.
- Address your contact with the appropriate level of formality and make sure you spelled their name correctly.
- Spell check - emails with typos are simply not taken as seriously.
- Read your email out loud to ensure the tone is that which you desire. Try to avoid relying on formatting for emphasis; rather choose the words that reflect your meaning instead. A few additions of the words "please" and "thank you" go a long way!
- Be sure you are including all relevant details or information necessary to understand your request or point of view. Generalities can many times cause confusion.
- Are you using proper sentence structure? First word capitalised with appropriate punctuation? Multiple instances of !!! or ??? are perceived as rude or condescending.
- If your email is emotionally charged, walk away from the computer and wait to reply. Review the Sender's

- If you bold your type, know you are bolding your statement and it will be taken that way by the other side.
- Do not use patterned backgrounds. Makes your email harder to read.
- Stay away from fancy fonts – only the standard fonts are on all computers.
- Use emoticons sparingly to ensure your tone and intent are clear.
- Typing your emails in all small case gives the perception of lack of education or laziness.
- Refrain from using multiple font colours in one email. It makes your email harder to view and can add to your intent being misinterpreted.
- Use formatting sparingly. Instead try to rely on choosing the most accurate words possible to reflect your tone and avoid misunderstandings in the process.

Email Attachments

- When sending large attachments, always "zip" or compress them before sending.
- Never send large attachments without notice! Always ask what would be the best time to send them first.
- Never open an attachment from someone you don't know.
- Be sure your virus and spyware programs are up to date and include scanning of your emails and attachments both incoming and outgoing.
- It is better to spread multiple attachments over several emails rather than attaching them all to one email to avoid clogging the pipeline.

- Make sure the other side has the same software as you before sending attachments or they may not be able to open your attachment. Use PDF when possible.

Email Forwarding

- Don't forward emails that say to do so—no matter how noble the cause may be, don't. Most are hoaxes.
- If someone asks you to refrain from forwarding emails they have that right and you shouldn't get mad or take it personally.
- When forwarding email, if you cannot take the time to type a personal comment to the person you are forwarding to—then don't bother.
- Don't forward anything without editing out all the forwarding >>>>, other email addresses, headers and commentary from all the other forwarders.
- Be careful when forwarding email on political or controversial issues. The recipient may not appreciate this.

Business Email

- Think of your business email as though it was on your business letterhead and you'll never go wrong!
- If you cannot respond to an email promptly, at the very least email back confirming your receipt and when the sender can expect your response.
- Emailing site owners about your product or service through the site form is still spam. Ask them if they want more info first!
- When replying to emails always respond promptly and edit out unnecessary information from the post you are responding to.

- Formality is in place as a courtesy and reflects respect. Assume the highest level of formality with new email contacts until the relationship dictates otherwise. Refrain from getting too informal too soon in your email communications.
- Never send anyone an email they need to unsubscribe from when they didn't subscribe in the first place!
- Be very careful how you use Reply to All and Cc: in a business environment.
- Never send business attachments outside of business hours and confirm that the format in which you can send can be opened by the other side.

IM, Blackberry

- With IM and Chat, try not to be overly cryptic or your meaning can be misread.
- Use Instant Messaging (IM) for casual topics or informational briefs. IM is not the place for serious topics or confrontational issues.
- Start by always asking if the person you are IMing is available and if it is a good time to chat. Refrain from IMing during meetings or when your attention is required.
- Practice communicating briefly and succinctly.
- Use IM for casual topics or informational briefs. Serious topics are not for IM.
- IMing is not an excuse to forget your grade school education.
- If you are not a smooth multi-tasker, do not continue multiple IM sessions and leave folks hanging while you communicate with others.
- Learn how to use the features of your IM program.

Specifically your "busy" and "away" message features.
- Never IM under an alias to take a peek at friends' or associates' activities.
- Take into consideration who you are communicating with to determine the acronyms and emoticons that should be used - if at all.

And finally... ***Type unto others as you would have them type unto you!***

ACADEMIC WRITING

Academic writing in English is linear, which means it has one central point or theme with every part contributing to the main line of argument, without digressions or repetitions. Its objective is to inform rather than entertain. As well as this it is in the standard written form of the language. There are **8 main features of academic writing** that are often discussed. Academic writing is to some extent: **complex, formal, objective, explicit, hedged, and responsible.** It uses **language precisely and accurately**.

Complexity

Written language is relatively more complex than spoken language. Written language has longer words, lexically it has a more varied vocabulary. It uses more noun-based phrases than verb-based phrases. Written texts are shorter and the language has more grammatical complexity, including more subordinate clauses and more passives.

Written language is grammatically more complex than spoken language. It has more subordinate clauses, more "that/to" complement clauses, more long sequences of prepositional phrases, more attributive adjectives and more passives than spoken language.

Common features in academic written texts:
<u>Noun-based phrases</u>, <u>Subordinate clauses/embedding</u>, <u>Complement clauses</u>, <u>Sequences of prepositional phrases</u>, <u>Participles</u>, <u>Passive verbs</u>, <u>Lexical density</u>, <u>Lexical complexity</u>, <u>Nominalisation</u>, <u>Attributive adjectives</u>

Formality

Academic writing is relatively formal. In general this means that in an essay you should avoid colloquial words and expressions. The main difference is the grammar, not the vocabulary.

Spoken	Written
Whenever I'd visited there before, I'd ended up feeling that it would be futile if I tried to do anything more.	Every previous visit had left me with a sense of the futility of further action on my part.
The cities in Libya had once been peaceful, but they changed when people became violent.	Violence changed the face of once peaceful Libyan cities.
Because the technology has improved it is less risky than it used to be when you install them at the same time, and it doesn't cost so much either.	Improvements in technology have reduced the risks and high costs associated with simultaneous installation.
The people in the colony rejoiced when it was promised that things would change in this way.	Opinion in the colony greeted the promised change with enthusiasm.

Precision

In academic writing, facts and figures are given precisely. In academic writing you need to be precise when you use information, dates or figures. Do not use "a lot of people" when you can say "50 million people".

Objectivity

Written language is in general objective rather than personal. It therefore has fewer words that refer to the writer or the reader. This means that the main emphasis should be on the information that you want to give and the arguments you want to make, rather than you. Academic writing tends to use nouns (and adjectives), rather than verbs (and adverbs).

Don't write:" In my opinion, this a very interesting study."

Write: "This is a very interesting study."

Avoid "you" to refer to the reader or people in general.

Don't write: "You can easily forget how different life was 50 years ago."

Write: "It is easy to forget how difficult life was 50 years ago."

Explicitness

Academic writing is explicit about the relationships in the text. Furthermore, it is the responsibility of the writer in English to make it clear to the reader how the various parts of the text are related. These connections can be made explicit by the use of different signalling words. Academic writing is explicit in several ways.

Accuracy

Academic writing uses vocabulary accurately. Most subjects have words with narrow specific meanings. Linguistics distinguishes clearly between "phonetics" and "phonemics"; general English does not.

In academic writing you need to be accurate in your use of vocabulary. Do not confuse, for example, "phonetics" and "phonology" or "grammar" with "syntax". Choose the correct word, for example, "meeting", "assembly", "gathering" or "conference"

Or

from: "money", "cash", "currency", "capital" or "funds".

Hedging

In any kind of academic writing you do, it is necessary to make decisions about your stance on a particular subject, or the strength of the claims you are making. Different subjects prefer to do this in different ways.

A technique common in certain kinds of academic writing is known by linguists as a 'hedge'.

It is often believed that academic writing, particularly scientific writing, is factual, simply to convey facts and information. However it is now recognised that an important feature of academic writing is the concept of cautious language, often called "hedging" or "vague language". In other words, it is necessary to make decisions about your stance on a particular subject, or the strength of the claims you are making. Different subjects prefer to do this in different ways.

Language used in hedging:

1. Introductory verbs:	e.g. seem, tend, look like, appear to be, think, believe, doubt, be sure, indicate, suggest
2. Certain lexical verbs	e.g. believe, assume, suggest
3. Certain modal verbs:	e.g. will, must, would, may, might, could
4. Adverbs of frequency	e.g. often, sometimes, usually
5. Modal adverbs	e.g. certainly, definitely, clearly, probably, possibly, perhaps, conceivably,
6. Modal adjectives	e.g. certain, definite, clear, probable, possible
7. Modal nouns	e.g. assumption, possibility, probability
8. That clauses	e.g. It could be the case that e.g. It might be suggested that e.g. There is every hope that
9. To-clause + adjective	e.g. It may be possible to obtain e.g. It is important to develop e.g. It is useful to study

Responsibility

In academic writing you must be responsible for, and must be able to provide evidence and justification for, any claims you make. You are also responsible for demonstrating an understanding of any source texts you use. This is done by paraphrasing and summarising what you read and acknowledging the source of this information or ideas by a system of citation.

ESSAYS

The Six P's

- Pleasant Appearance
- Proper Selection of Subject
- Planning
- Proportion
- Perspicuity
- Persuasiveness.

Pleasant Appearance

- Do write legibly and without crossings-out. Penmanship is important.
- Do indent for every paragraph, including the first.
- Do keep a left-hand margin, and try to keep a right-hand one too, making this as even as possible, for a jagged ending of lines looks most unattractive.

Proper Selection of Subject

- In examinations candidates are usually allowed a fairly wide choice of essay subject. Choose one that suits you.
- There are generally five types of essays: Narrative, Descriptive, Reflective, Argumentative and Expository.
- Find out which kinds you can do best. Don't plunge into discussions of scientific and technical subjects without a detailed knowledge.
- Don't attempt artistic description if you are deficient in imagination.

- Be sure to read the titles carefully and notice any qualifying words or unusual expressions.
- If you don't quite understand a quotation or proverb set as a title, or feel there is some ambiguity about it, don't choose it.
- Make sure you understand the meaning of your title perfectly. Having once selected your subject, abide by your choice.

Planning

- The four essential stages in the creation of an essay are: Thinking, Arranging, Writing, and Revising.
- Always have rough paper.
- Write your ideas down on this paper first.
- Always make a plan (a general outline or scheme, a skeleton framework).
- Don't sit thinking too long; get your ideas down on paper quickly.
- Plan your time too and practice writing to time-limits. Spend say 1/6 of the time allowed on thinking about it and drawing up your outline, 3/4 of the time on writing it, and 1/12 of the time for revision and correction.
- It is important to keep enough time for a final reading, but be careful not to have too much time left or you will be tempted to add on after-thoughts to an essay already finished and revised.

Proportion

- Your essay must have a beginning, middle and an end.
- Make a good introduction -not too lengthy or you will exhaust your theme in the opening paragraph.

- Pay attention to 'the architecture of composition'.
- Good paragraphing is vital.
- Break up your essay into paragraphs, following your rough plan.
- Vary the length of your paragraphs-a short "sandwich paragraph' between two longer ones can be very effective.
- Arrange your paragraphs properly-don't skip backwards and forwards.
- Each idea should follow on in logical order, each paragraph advancing your essay and the succession of paragraphs corresponding with the sense, so that any alteration in the order of paragraphs would dislocate the whole unity of the essay.

Perspicuity

- Don't mess and muddle; get your thoughts straight before you write.
- Be lucid and clear.
- Perspicuity implies simplicity, brevity and precision.
- Write in direct and plain English.
- Write with economy and accuracy, for perspicuity, like that other great virtue in writing, sincerity, implies "saying what you mean, and meaning what you say".
- Use no words that you do not understand, measuring your epithets, never repeating phrases from books without.

Persuasiveness

- To charm your reader or examiner your writing must be persuasive.

- Do not be stale but fresh
- Be original
- Do not be wooden but lively and imaginative
- Do not be monotonous but varied
- Do not be spineless but vigorous
- Do not be faded but vivid.
- Use concrete and specific images, not abstract and general ones
- Appeal to the senses of sight, sound, smell, taste and touch
- Use similes, metaphors and other figures of speech to stimulate the reader's imagination-in short, study suitable interest devices to attract, impress and hold the attention.

Figures of Speech

Figures of speech are vivid and striking images that will enrich your writing considerably. Here is a list of some of the most important figures of speech in English. These, if correctly and imaginatively used, can help to make your style more lively and interesting.

1. *Simile.* This is a very common figure of speech in English. It is a *comparison,* showing similarity between one thing and another, and usually introduced by the word *as* of *like.*

    e.g. Her tears fell like rain.
         He is as patient as a sheep.
         You look like a ghost!

Some idiomatic similes in common use in English:

as good as gold	as clear as crystal
as right as rain	as fit as a fiddle

as fat as butter	as heavy as lead
as thin as a rake	as light as a feather
as dry as a bone	as fresh as a daisy
as sharp as a needle	as pretty as a picture
as brave as a lion	as happy as a lark
as sound as a bell	as cool as a cucumber
as bold as brass	as busy as a bee or bees
as cold as ice	as ugly as sin
as hard as nails	as brown as a berry
as slippery as an eel	as true as steel
as hungry as a hunter	as stiff as a poker
as drunk as a lord	as dead as a door nail
as sober as a judge	as old as the hills
as poor as a church mouse	as strong as a horse
as rich as Croesus	as weak as water

2. *Metaphor*. Here the comparison is not introduced by *as* or *like*. Instead of saying "He is as brave as a lion", we say "He is a lion". Instead of *resemblance* we have *identification*.

e.g. He is just a poor fish.
Here is the fruit of my labour.
He is a tower of strength.
She was cut off in the flower of her youth and beauty.
This shop is a real gold-mine.

Many metaphors are in common use in English.

a ray of hope	a flash of inspiration
the fire of passion	a flow of words
the depths of despair	the dawn of history
the heights of happiness	to bombard with questions

the school of life	to be consumed with curiosity
the wind of change	to launch a campaign
the book of nature	to steer clear of
the key to the mystery	to strike a note
the heart of the matter	to overflow with ideas
the root of the trouble	to put up a good fight
	to burst into tears.

Be careful: Don't *mix* your metaphors by confusing your comparisons.

e.g. Life is not always a bed of roses–it is sometimes stormy. (A flower-bed cannot become stormy!)

3. *Personification.* This is a form of metaphorical speech in which inanimate or abstract things and ideas are treated as if they were human *persons*. Thus we speak of time as "Father Time" or the moon as "Lady Moon" or spring as a young girl and winter as an old man.

Love is blind.
Death is no respecter of persons.
The winds are whispering.

4. *Contrast (Antithesis).* This is the opposite of metaphor. By balancing two *opposing* words or ideas against each other a vivid sense of *contrast* and *difference* is obtained.

Speech is silver; silence is golden.
To err is human; to forgive, divine.
He was a good husband but a bad father.
God made the country and man made the town.

5. *Paradox.* This is also a form of contrast – the presentation of truth in a form apparently self-contradictory and absurd.

Only the man who has known fear can be truly brave.

We must die in order to live.
Vision is the art of seeing things invisible.

6. *Oxymoron.* Here the contrast is sharper and the contradictory words are put as close together as possible. It is a kind of condensed paradox.

a wise fool
an open secret
a cheerful pessimism
bitter-sweet memories.

7. *Epigram.* This is a short witty saying, often containing a paradoxical idea.

"Fools rush in where angels fear to tread." (*Pope*)
"The child is father of the man." (*Wordsworth*)
"A favourite has no friend." (*Gray*)

8. *Transferred Epithet.* This is an adjective placed before a word to which it does not really apply.

"The ploughman homeward plods his *weary way.*" (*Gray*)
(The ploughman is weary, not the way.)

Transferred epithets are found in such phrases as:

a sleepless night	the condemned cell
melancholy news	a happy time
a burning question	as anxious letter

9. *Exaggeration (Hyperbole)*. This is the use of ***overstatement*** for the sake of effect. When you say to a person "I haven't seen you for ages" you don't really mean "ages", and when you say "he ran like the wind" you don't seriously think that he was as fast as the wind-you are merely exaggerating to make a vivid impression.

I've heard that joke hundreds of times.
I thought that I would die of laughing.
It's so cold and we are absolutely frozen!
"All the perfumes of Arabia will not sweeten this little hand." (*Shakespeare.*)

10. *Understatement.* There are two main kinds of understatement. One is when we try to *soften* unpleasant things, e.g. by calling death "sleep", or a lie "an inaccuracy" This is called by the Greek word *euphemism.*

Her husband fell asleep (or *passes on* or *passes away*) last week (- *died*).

Sometimes I think you are a stranger to the truth (-*a liar*).

The other kind of understatement is used intentionally to give greater positive emphasis to the idea. This is called by the Greek word ***Litotes,*** and it is very common in English.

Understatement		*Real Meaning*
not bad	=	very good
not uncommon	=	very common
not a few	=	many
not a little	=	much
quite good	=	excellent

11. *Climax.* *This* means "a ladder" or "series of steps" and is the presentation of a number of ideas to give a gradual increase in intensity, so that the last idea is the strongest of all.

    e.g. "I came, I saw, I conquered."
        "What a piece of work is man? How infinite in faculties! (*Shakespeare*)

12. *Anti-climax.* This is just the opposite: the ideas descend in order of importance. It is often used in humorous writing.

He lost his wife, his children-and his purse.
He is a great philosopher, a fine teacher and he plays tennis well too.

13. *Onomatopoeia*. This means simply the formation of words by *the imitation of sounds*. The sense echoes the sound.

The *buzzing* of bees.
The *patter* of rain.
The sound of the *cuckoo*.
The water *dripped* from the tap.

Bang, splash, crash, bump, thud, swish, crack, gram, whisper, scream, hiss – All these words are onomatopoeic words- and there are hundreds more. Try to make your own lists of vivid sound-words.

14. *Alliteration*. This is also to do with sound, and is the frequent repetition of the same letter or sound in words.

Pink pills for pale people.
Stay the summer in the sunny south.

The taste for alliteration is very strong in the English language, and besides the alliterative similes "good as gold", "bold as brass" and so on, we have hundreds of little alliterative phrases in everyday use.

chop and change	the lap of luxury
sink or swim	make or mar
part and parcel	do or die
first and foremost	fact or fiction
last but not least	spick and span
slowly but surely	the why and wherefore
fast and furious	friend or foe

short and sweet	safe and sound
from top to toe	neither rhyme nor reason
through thick and thin	toss and turn

There are also *alliterative proverbs*:
Waste not, want not.
A miss is as good as a mile.
Every dog has his day.
Look before you leap.

SOME ONE-WORD SUBSTITUTES FOR SENTENCES

- *Antiseptic:* that which prevents animal and vegetable substances from rotting, decaying or decomposing.
- *Abdicate:* to give up or renounce a throne voluntarily.
- *Autobiography:* life of a person written by himself.
- *Acclimatize:* to accustom oneself to a foreign climate.
- *Accomplice:* a partner in a crime or guilt.
- *Arbitrator:* a person chosen by parties who have a controversy or quarrel to settle their difference.
- *Aggressor:* one who commits the first act of attack, offence or hostility.
- *Ambiguous:* capable of being understood in two or more possible senses; therefore, of doubtful and indefinite meaning.
- *Accessible:* that which can be easily approached, influenced or obtained.
- *Anarchist:* one who believes in no law, government or supreme power, and therefore incites disorder in a state.
- *Autocrat:* a monarch who holds and exercises the power

of government by claim of absolute right, not subject to any restriction.
- *Atheist:* one who does not believe in the existence of god.
- *Blasphemy:* words uttered impiously and contemptuously against God.
- *Bigot:* one who is blindly and obstinately devoted to a particular faith, creed or party.
- *Bibliophile:* a person who is a great lover of books (especially a collector of rare books).
- *Bilingual:* able to express oneself in two languages.
- *Cosmopolitan:* a person who is nowhere a stranger and feels at home all over the world (a citizen of the world). Also used adjectivally-free from local or national prejudices and attachments.
- *Circumlocution:* the use of many words to express an idea which might be expressed by a few.
- *Contemporaries:* those living in the same period (Coleridge and Wordsworth were contemporaries).
- *Compatriot:* belonging to the same country and having same interests and feelings.
- *Connoisseur:* one who is well versed in any subject; a critical judge of any art, particularly fine arts.
- *Desecrate:* to violate the sacred character of anything.
- *Deputize:* to appoint some one, or an agent or representative, to act in one's place.
- *Distort:* to twist anything out of its natural shape or position.
- *Deadlock:* such a complicated state of affairs between two (or more) parties that brings all action or progress to a standstill.
- *Democracy:* government of the people, by the people, for the people.

- *Dotage:* extreme old age when a person behaves in a childish and foolish manner.
- *Digress:* to wander away from the main point, (to beat about the bush, to be wide of the mark.)
- *Expatriate:* to send out of one's native country.
- *Expurgate:* to exclude all objectionable matter (from some book or document).
- *Exhaustive:* full and clear in detail.
- *Edible:* that which is fit to be eaten as food.
- *Eligible:* proper or qualified to be selected for any office or duty.
- *Egoist:* a person who thinks or speaks too much of himself.
- *Extempore:* performed without previous study or preparation.
- *Epilogue:* a speech or short poem addressed to the spectators by one of the actors, after the conclusion of a drama.
- *Explicit:* (a statement) plain in language which can be easily understood.
- *Endemic:* a disease which is peculiar to a locality or a class of persons.
- *Eternal:* that which will last for ever and never perish.
- *Ephemeral:* anything that is of a passing nature and has a short-lived existence.
- *Extradite:* to deliver a criminal to the authorities of the country from which he has come.
- *Feasible:* capable of being done, executed or effected.
- *Fanatic:* a person who is wild and extravagant in opinion, particularly in religious matters.
- *Fatalist:* one who believes in fate or chance.
- *Feminist:* one who believes in offering equal opportunities to women in all spheres.

- *Harangue:* a noisy and bombastic speech addressed to a large assembly.
- *Hereditary:* descended or capable of descending from father to son.
- *Honorary:* an office for which no salary is paid.
- *Inaugural:* (A speech) delivered at the opening ceremony of any function.
- *Instigate:* to urge somebody to do something wrong or wicked.
- *Interpolate:* to insert new matter in a book or manuscript.
- *Imposter:* a person who assumes a character or titles not his own for the purpose of deceiving others.
- *Irretrievable:* that which cannot be recovered (a loss etc.)
- *Inevitable:* that which cannot be avoided.
- *Idiosyncrasy:* a peculiarity of temperament which distinguishes an individual from others.
- *Imperceptible:* that which cannot be seen or perceived by the senses.
- *Inanimate:* that which possesses no life or spirit.
- *Indictment:* a formal written charge against a person for some crime or offence.
- *Innovation:* introduction of something new in any field.
- *Incredible:* that which cannot be believed.
- *Infallible:* that which is incapable or error or fault.
- *Impracticable:* that which cannot be put into practice.
- *Illicit:* that which is not permitted by law.
- *Inimitable:* that which cannot be imitated.
- *Insolvent:* (A debtor) who is unable to pay his debts.
- *Insoluble:* that which cannot be solved.
- *Indefatigable:* incapable of feeling tired or exhausted.
- *Iconoclast:* a breaker of images, or conventions.

- *Inept:* that is out of place (a remark, etc.,)
- *Illiterate:* incapable or reading or writing.
- *Inaudible:* that which cannot be heard.
- *Irrefragable:* that which cannot be answered, or overthrown (an argument or evidence).
- *Itinerant:* one who travels from place to place; particularly a preacher.
- *Invulnerable:* that which cannot be wounded, injured or assailed.
- *Idolatry:* the worship of idols or images.
- *Illegible:* that which cannot be easily read (a document or a manuscript).
- *Insatiable:* that which cannot be satisfied (thirst or curiosity).
- *Insuperable:* that which cannot be overcome.
- *Intermedia:* one who acts between two or more parties, to settle differences.
- *Irreproachable:* that which is free from blame.
- *Loquacious:* talkative.
- *Migratory:* (birds or animals) moving from one region to another.
- *Misconstrue:* to interpret in a wrong sense.
- *Maiden speech:* the first public speech delivered by a person.
- *Misogynist:* a person who hates women.
- *Misanthrope:* a hater of mankind.
- *Misologist:* own who hates learning or knowledge.
- *Maxim:* an established principle of practical wisdom.
- *Naturalize:* to confer on a person the rights and privileges of a state to which he does not belong.
- *Notorious:* with an evil reputation.
- *Neologism:* a new word coined by an author.

- *Ostracize:* to banish from society, to cast out of a social or political favour.
- *Oligarchy:* government in which the supreme power is placed in the hands of a small body of men.
- *Octagon:* a plane figure having eight sides and eight angles.
- *Obsolete:* no longer in use (word or custom).
- *Omnipotent:* possessing unlimited powers.
- *Optimist:* one who always looks on the bright side of things, or takes a hopeful view of life (the opposite of a *pessimist*).
- *Octogenarian:* a person eighty years of age.
- *Pioneer:* one who leads others in any field.
- *Portable:* that which can be easily carried from one place to another.
- *Pseudonym:* a fictitious name assumed by an author.
- *Philanthropist:* one who loves mankind and seeks to promote the good of others.
- *Panacea:* a remedy which cures all diseases.
- *Polyglot:* one who understands many languages.
- *Polygamy:* the practice of having several wives at the same time.
- *Potable:* that which can be drunk.
- *Polygon:* a plain figure having many sides.
- *Pacifist:* a person who believes in the total abolition of war.
- *Polysyllable:* a word of many syllables.
- *Polytheist:* one who believes in many gods.
- *Parasite:* one who lives at another's expense; derives benefit from somebody else's labours.
- *Posthumous:* (a book) published after the death of its author.

- *Plagiarist:* one who steals from another writer's compositions and offers them as his own.
- *Quadruped:* an animal having four feet.
- *Red Tape:* excessive use of official formalities which causes unnecessary delay.
- *Simultaneously:* occurring or happening at the same time.
- *Slander:* false report maliciously uttered to injure a person's reputation.
- *Smuggle:* to import or export goods illegally without the payment of custom duties.
- *Sinecure:* a post with little work but high salary.
- *Stoic:* a person who has trained himself to be indifferent to pleasure or pain.
- *Sacrilege:* violation of that which is holy and sacred.
- *Tangible:* Perceptible by touch, definite, clear and intelligible, not elusive or visionary.
- *Teetotaler:* a person who does not take any intoxicating drinks.
- *Tell-tale:* one who talks about another's private affairs and secrets.
- *Titular:* only in name, without any power or authority (held only by virtue of a title).
- *Transient:* of a very short duration.
- *Truant:* a student who absents himself without permission from a school or a college by running away. The idiom is to *play truant (from)*.
- *Usurer:* one who lends money on high rates of interest.
- *Voluntary:* acting on one's free will.
- *Veteran:* a person who has long experience of any service or occupation.
- *Verbose:* that is full of more words than necessary.

- *Valetudinarian:* a person who always thinks that he is ill.
- *Zoology:* the science of animal life.

Steps in the Writing Process

- Step 1 - **RESEARCH**
- Step 2 - **PLAN**
- Step 3 - **DRAFT**
- Step 4 - **REVISE**
- Step 5 - **PROOF**

Step 1: Research

Research is the gathering of ideas and information. This is the step where you answer the "who, when, where, what, and how of the issue". Since we gather information in different ways, you must find the system which best suits you and your task. This means that as you gather ideas, you must keep in mind both your purpose and your audience. Gather as many ideas as you can. Use all possible sources. It is easier to throw out ideas that you don't need than it is to go back and do more research. Once you have the ideas you need, you will continue to the planning stage.

Step 2: Plan

The planning step is where you take all the information you've gathered and put it into a logical order. Start by placing your ideas into groups. The product that results is the outline. From this ordering, develop a controlling idea. A controlling idea is a single declarative sentence which presents both your topic and your position about that topic.

Once you have developed the controlling idea, add your supporting paragraphs. What you have is a rough plan or outline. Now you're ready to write your first draft.

Step 3. Develop A Draft

The draft is the bridge between your idea and the expression of it. Write your draft quickly and concentrate only on getting your ideas down on paper. Don't worry about punctuation and spelling. Use your outline to develop your draft. State your controlling idea (the bottom line) early and follow the order you've already developed. When you have the ideas down and you're satisfied with the sequence, you need to put the product into the correct writing format. This may result in your re-writing sections of your draft so that it fits the appropriate format. After you complete the formatting of your draft, put it aside. It is a good idea to get away from the paper for a while before you start to revise.

Step 4. Revise the Draft

Revising is looking at the material through the eyes of your audience. Read the paper as if you have never seen it before. Find where you need to put in transitions; look for places that need more evidence. This will help you decide if you need to add enclosures or add information depending on the type of written product you are developing. You now revise your draft making the changes you've noted.

Step 5. Proof

Now you are ready to proof your draft. At this point concentrate on the format, grammar, mechanics, and usage. You may want to have someone else read it. Sometimes others can find errors you can't because you are too close to the product. When you finish, write the final version, making the corrections. Your product is now complete.

Some Tips for Better Letter

Make up your mind today to answer mail promptly and to become a first-class letter writer.

Here are some tips for better letters to your family and friends.

1. Whenever you feel like or are inspired to write to a friend, do it. Don't delay.
2. Don't wait for an immortal first line. Start writing.
3. Fill your letters with news: what you're doing, friends you have seen, interesting incidents, lively questions. News is what makes a letter.
4. Let your style be informal, punchy, filled with images.
5. Try to answer questions you know your friend is interested in and, is you do so, make every word count.
6. Avoid phrases that you hear time and time again. Examples: "Hope you are fine," "With these words I end my letter."
7. If you are not sure whether you should write a letter or not, write it, keep it aside for a day or so, and then decide.
8. Letters make a difference. You will be surprised what one letter can do: the useful information it can convey, the change it can bring about, the encouragement it can give.

How to Write An Application Letter

An application letter consists of two parts: (1) Your personal history or resume, and (2) a covering letter.

Cover Letter

The purpose of this letter, like the resume, is to make prospective employer want to meet you. The letter should introduce you to the employer, highlight experience relevant to the organisation's needs and manifest your interest in the firm and post.

Address your letter, if possible, to a specific person by name and title unless an advertisement gives only a box number.

Make your letter brief. Tell how you learned of the employer and why you are interested in the organisation. If someone who knows the employer has referred you, mention that person's name. Close the letter by indicating your desire to have an interview.

Cover Letter Format

First paragraph: Identifies the job and you. This is brief, to the point, direct.

Second paragraph: Identifies some special skills, qualities or experience that makes you a very suitable candidate.

Third paragraph: Express your desire for an interview.

How to Write Your Personal History or Resume

1. Know the purpose of your resume
2. Back up your qualities and strengths
3. Make sure to use the right keywords
4. Use effective titles
5. Proofread it twice
6. Use bullet points
7. Where are you going
8. Put the most important information first
9. Attention to the typography
10. Do not include "no kidding" information
11. Explain the benefits of your skills
12. Avoid negativity
13. Achievements instead of responsibilities
14. No pictures
15. Use numbers
16. One resume for each employer
17. Identify the problems of the employer
18. You don't need to list all your work experiences
19. Go with what you got
20. Sell yourself
21. Don't include irrelevant information
22. No lies, please
23. Keep the salary in mind
24. Analyse job ads
25. One or two pages
26. Use action verbs
27. Use a good printer
28. Update your resume regularly
29. Mention who you worked with

30. No scattered information
31. No pronouns
32. Don't forget the basics

The Key Factors

A resume is a document by which you 'sell' yourself. It should be so arranged as to emphasise your strengths. While there is no single way of writing a resume, here are some tips that you may find useful.

1. State your career objective and include all training, experiences and skills that are in line with it.
2. Sell yourself. Emphasise your accomplishments, skills, and levels of responsibility attained; all this however, without exaggeration.
3. Put first things first. The important items belong at the top. Within each item arrange the information with your career goal in mind.
4. Use reverse chronological order. When items are listed by date, put the most recent first.
5. Write in an action-oriented style. Use action verbs to highlight what you have done.
6. Make it brief. Omit unnecessary words and phrases: "I", "my duties consisted of"; delete irrelevant.
7. Be accurate. No mistakes in spelling or grammar.
8. Make it spotless and attractive; well centred and no crowding.

Resume Sections

Career Objective:

Education:

Related Qualifications:

Other Training:

Related Work Experience:

Additional Experience:

Publications:

Honours/Awards:

Extracurricular Activities:

An Effective Cover Letter

Your resume can be very impressive. But if your cover letter isn't equally impressive, it's entirely possible that your resume will never get read. First impressions are lasting impressions. Most people spend about twenty seconds reading a cover letter, so it has to make your case clearly and effectively.

5 Tips

1. Be brief and to the point.
2. Make no mistake about it.
3. Use a word processor.
4. Avoid fancy fonts and colours.
5. Keep it short.

How to Outline

If you want to draw up a plan or project, to write a speech, or to write an examination or even a letter, or to takes notes well in class, these and a hundred other tasks are helped by an outline.

What does outlining mean? To outline means to show the framework, to expose the structure of a communication.

How do you make an outline? Basically, outlining consists of four steps: collecting, analysing, classifying and subordinating data.

1. *Collect Data:* Before beginning to write, let us say, a report or a speech, read yourself full on the subject. Read the latest, read the best. Make notes.
2. *Analyze the Data:* Look over the materials you have

collected. Decide what the scope of your report or speech will be. Decide which of the data you will use, which you will not use because it is not connected with your purpose.

3. *Classify the Data:* Divide the material you will use into classes or groups: e.g. if you will speak of mangoes, cashews, pecans, lichees, apples and walnuts, divide into

   Nuts: Cashews, pecans, walnuts.
   Fruits: Apples, Lichees, Mangoes.

4. *Organize the data:* According to your purpose, put an order in the data you will present. What group of material will I present first? Which last? What is most important? What least important?

How to Write An Effective Report

The Boss generally glances at the first page: If it is less than half a page but it contains a precise statement of the problem investigated or project assigned they are happy. They turn the page and there on one page they have a concise summary of the whole report: the major facts, the conclusions these facts lead to, the action recommended on the basis of the conclusions; all this on one page and they find it easy to comprehend.

An effective report has six parts in the following order:

Parts	Function
1. Introduction	Statement of problem or task (half page or less)
2. Summary	One page condensation

3. Body	Method, significant facts and details
4. Conclusion	Meaning of facts given in Body
5. Recommendation	Alternatives and alternative recommended
6. Appendix	Tables and less relevant information

NOTE: Don't forget the one-page summary: TOPS - The One Page System.

How to Write A Book Review

Writing a good book review can sometimes seem challenging but try to think of it this way: when you rave about an amazing book to a friend you can easily go on for hours on the subject, quoting your favourite passages, examining how it related to you, the amazing recipes or photographs, and so on. A book review is the same thing but concise and with a little more forethought and organisation.

Read the entire book cover to cover. Put it down. Muse over it for a few days or even a week or two. What sticks with you? Certain passages? Do you see food, drink, people, society, or cultures in a new light? Have certain culinary techniques, dishes or ingredients worked their way into your everyday life? Has your writing style altered a bit? Did the pictures teach you a new photographic technique? These are the things your readers will want to know and will make for an interesting post.

Relate to your readers your history with the book. You may have just been lured in by a pretty cover or found it buried in your mother's bookshelves. Your story with the book is an important and engaging part of the review and gives your post personality.

Give a short history of the author and the book itself. This can often be found in an author's biography or preface section. This short history helps frame the book placing it into context and giving it an important first impression.

Explain why the book is unique. For example, how does the author explain the use of ingredients in baking better than other authors? By setting the author and subject apart from the overcrowded world of food literature you detail their importance.

Using examples is a great way to get your point across. If you say a particular author's writing style is unique, provide a passage that exemplifies it. Afterwards show your readers what stands out, why they should take note, and how it affected you.

Remember the author's intended audience. You may not be the type of person the author meant the book to be read by, so you may not enjoy it the same way others might. Liking a book and appreciating the talent and composition behind it are different things.

Don't give away the meat of the book. Don't tell who killed the cheesemonger, or explain every recipe. Briefly cover the main point/plot/purpose or highlight a section or two but let your readers discover the book for themselves.

If you're reviewing a cookbook try as many recipes as possible. Five recipes is usually a good number to shoot for as it gives you a chance to sample various dishes and write a comprehensive review, however the more recipes you try the better. You don't have to mention every single dish, but it gives you choices for reference and you can state with confidence if they worked or not, and why.

Don't like the book? Don't just slam it with a few one-liners, but rather explain the flaws of the book clearly using facts and personal experiences.

The Pattern

Many book reviews are more interesting reading than the books themselves. Reading book reviews, moreover, is a marvelous way of keeping yourself up-to-date on developments. For these and other reasons, a well-written review is a distinct service to readers. If you are writing a book review, here's how to go about it:

1. State the name of the book, author, publisher, place and year of publication, number of pages, and price.
2. Remember your task is not to summarise, but evaluate. Avoid statements such as: "In the third chapter the author talks about." Your contribution is evaluation, not summary.
3. Understand the book thoroughly before you attempt to evaluate it. Don't attribute positions or views to authors which they do not maintain.
4. In your critical review, answer the following questions:
   a. What is the purpose of the author in writing the book?
   (Look well at preface, introduction)
   b. Does the author accomplish this purpose?
   c. Do you think there was a need for such a book? Every book should have a reason for existence: some new contribution or addition to work already done.

d. What are the strong points of the book? Weak points? Illustrate.
   e. Are there any particular positions, concepts, or conclusions that you thought particularly worthwhile or, perhaps, questionable?
   f. Do you have any comments on the organisation, printings, or lay-out of the book?
   g. Would you recommend the book? To whom *specifically*? Why?
5. Be scrupulously fair but be honest. Undeserved praise serves no purpose. Honest criticism, even if negative, spurs the author to greater effort.

   So become a reader of book reviews and when you write one, stay on target. The target is evaluation, criticism both negative and positive. Build up confidence and pride in you own judgement.

Many Faces of 'Only'

Only he said that he loved her
He only said that he loved her
He said only that he loved her
He said that only he loved her
He said that he only loved her
He said that he loved only her
He said that he loved her only

How to Write a News Release

1. Writing the Copy

What someone writes down and hands it to the editor

of a paper is called copy. The writing itself is much less important than the gathering of *facts*. News means what actually happened; what people did or said – not what they might have done-and the reporter must learn first of all to get the fact straight and to make up the report from facts and not from opinions and guesses.

2. Finding the Facts

A few experiences will impress any reporter with the importance of accuracy and completeness. Any journalist soon learns to get people identified and names spelled correctly. If a story comes to him as a rumour, it can't be used unless he is able to track it down to reliable source. Honest journalism is primarily a habit of looking first and last for facts. The one rule: 'when in doubt, leave it out'.

3. Putting the Facts in Order: the Lead Sentence

In arranging the facts you have gathered, there is one simple rule *about news stories*. The opening sentence, called *the lead* should carry the most important part of the news story. From it the rest of the story tapers down in importance like a 'who did what', when, where, how and why? The paragraph that follows can fill in the details, is so written that the editor can cut away everything except the lead and yet have a brief but complete news statement.

The story is told three times: telegraphically in the headlines, summarily but precisely in the space allowed in the following paragraphs. Your information should contain in itself enough drama to hold the reader's attention. If it doesn't it probably isn't news. The key is the inverted pyramid:

Tips on Writing a News Release

1. Make sure the information is newsworthy.
2. Tell the audience that the information is intended for them and why they should continue to read it.
3. Start with a brief description of the news, then distinguish who announced it, and not the other way around.
4. Ask yourself, "How are people going to relate to this and will they be able to connect?"
5. Make sure the first 10 words of your release are effective, as they are the most important.
6. Avoid excessive use of adjectives and fancy language.
7. Deal with the facts.
8. Provide as much Contact information as possible: Individual to Contact, address, phone, fax, email, Web site address.
9. Make sure you wait until you have something with enough substance to issue a release.
10. Make it as easy as possible for media representatives to do their jobs

How to Get Started on a Research Project

The word 'research' is an academic sounding word but all it means is finding out the truth about any matter. Here are the 5 Canons of research work.

1. *Read yourself full on the subject in question.*
   Your research should add something new and fill in some gap in the existing body of knowledge. So learn the present state of the 'art', go through the literature. Don't neglect encyclopedias. Aim to contribute something *new*.
2. *Formulate the question your project will answer.*
   All research should answer a question.
3. *Now list serially all the information or data needed to answer your question.*
   What information will I need to answer my question?
4. *Then go through the list of required information.*

How to Write a Letter to the Editor

Abuse thrives in secrecy. Media coverage helps end that secrecy. It also emboldens other victims and concerned members of the family to come forward. Therefore, one easy step survivors can take to help one another is to write letters to the editor (for publication) of newspapers. Here are some tips.

Be brief, be quick and leave your phone numbers. These are the three most important things to remember when writing letters to the editor.

Be brief, because there's a lot of competition for a small amount of space.

Be quick in writing because the best letter in the world won't get run if the newspaper gets it 3 or 4 weeks after the original article it refers to was printed.

Leave your number. Many papers won't print letters unless they can call the author to verify that he or she wrote it. So sign the letter, and leave both your day and evening phone number.

Other Tips:

1. **Use statistics sparingly.** They can get confusing and overwhelming very quickly.
2. **Mention an article already printed by the paper.** This dramatically increases the chances that your letter will be run.
3. **Remember your audience.** In most cases you're trying to sway the public, not your adversary. Therefore, you should take pains to seem moderate and fair. This doesn't mean you should be bland. But you should write with the average person in mind, and use phrases and arguments that resonate with them.
4. **A catchy first line is helpful.** Instead of "I'm writing to respond to the X editorial of August 3rd," try "As a gun owner, the August 3rd editorial left me wondering if X editorial writers live in the real world."
5. **Don't mention criticism that has been leveled against you** or your organisation. Avoid saying "I am not a crook, thief and a liar as reported in last week's X". Better to say "X readers wonder who's telling the truth in the controversy over___."
6. **Use short punchy sentences.** This makes it easier for the reader to follow your thinking and easier for the editor to cut your letter if necessary (and better to

have an edited version of your letter printed than none at all).
7. **It never hurts to send your letter via both fax and email.** Feel free to follow up with a phone call to make sure the appropriate person got your letter.

Editorials tell us what the news means—as the editor sees it. A letter to the Editor gives the reader a chance to say what the news means—as he or she sees it.

Writing a letter when it's not absolutely necessary makes it more likely that you'll do so when you must. You can frequently influence the opinions of many by doing so.

Tips

1. Give the reference
2. Begin immediately. Start your message with the first sentence. No run-up.
3. Be terse. Better for you to compress than the Editor.
4. Be assertive yet not aggressive.
5. Reason wins the day, not emotions. The Letters to the editor column is not an emotional junk box.
6. Do not attribute positions to the paper or writer that they do not hold. Check and double check.
7. Don't be surprised if the Editor edits, but complain if he or she changes the thrust.

How to Write a Grievance

In every organisation, even the best, injustices are done to individuals. Sometimes these injustices are done deliberately but in most cases they are not deliberate.

Write the facts. Write the facts in order. Write only the facts. And answer with facts the following 6 questions:

1. What is your name, ticket number, designation, section?
2. What happened?
3. When did it happen?
4. Where did it happen?
5. Why is it a grievance?
6. State your request.

Ten Tips for Writing a Grievance

- Limit details to basic information.
  Provide only enough information to identify the grievance so that management understands:
  a. what the basic problem is,
  b. what violations have occurred, and
  c. how the problem should be fixed (remedy).
- Don't include the union's argument, the union's evidence, or the union's justification for its position. Management could use this information to prepare a better case against the union.
- Don't limit contract violations.
  In stating WHY there is a grievance, use the phrase "violates the contract" and the words "including Article ..." when citing specific articles or sections in the contract. (By adding the word "including," you can always add additional violations of the agreement if they are found later.)
- Avoid personal remarks.
  The grievance states the UNION'S position, not your opinion or the grievant's opinion. Avoid the use of

phrases like "I think" or opinions about management officials.

- Don't limit the remedy.

  If you limit the remedy, you don't allow the union room to bargain on the grievance. You also might limit the union to something less than full compensation for the grievant by leaving out something you may remember later. This can be accomplished by using the general phrase "made whole in every way" and the word "including" when referring to specific remedies. (The general phrase "made whole in every way" means that the grievant should receive any and all losses due to management's action. This could include interest on money, wages, seniority, job rights, etc. whatever is due the grievant according to the contract. The word "including" allows you to add specific remedies later on, in writing or in oral arguments with management.)

- But just because you use the general phrase "made whole in every way" does not mean that an arbitrator or management will search out all the specific benefits management denied the grievant for you. It is up to YOU to list (verbally or in writing) any remedies not noted in the original written grievance.

- Consult with the grievant.

  Go over the written grievance. Explain the requested remedy and get the grievant's full understanding and agreement.

- Sign the grievance.

  Have the grievant sign the grievance. This gives the union the right to settle the grievance as it sees fit.

- Maintain solidarity.

  Explain the grievance to your members and be sure they understand and support your efforts.

- Communicate.
  Keep the grievant up to date on each action. Don't wait for him/her to come to you.
- Keep arbitration in mind.
  Prepare each case on the assumption that it may go to arbitration.

Writing Goal

Persons who achieve, generally have a special way of thinking. They constantly think of their goals, and why they are important to them. They imagine how they will feel if they succeed or if they fail. They look ahead to possible obstacles and helps, and get down to making action plans. After listing one writing goal in the box below, assess it for importance (I) and difficulty (D). Also check to see whether there is any conflict with any other goal of yours (C).

Writing Goal for the next six months.

	I	D	C

(Practice)

HOW TO WRITE A SPEECH

How to Write: A Memorable Speech: 10 TIPS

1. **Prepare Early.** Begin gathering material for your speech right away. As you learn more about your

topic, new ideas for writing and organizing it will automatically come to you.

2. **Be Audience-Centered.** Everything you write should be with the needs of the audience in mind. Aim all your efforts at helping the audience understand what you are saying.

3. **Start At The End First.** Write the conclusion of your talk right away. Decide what you want the audience to do or to think as a result of your speech. Then write the talk using that as a guide.

4. **Write For The Ear, Not The Eye.** Experienced writers know that every medium and project has its own language, cadence, style and structure. Don't write the speech to be read. You need to write your speech so when your audience hears it, they get it.

5. **Make Rough Drafts First And Polish Later.** Don't needlessly pressure yourself by trying to write the perfect speech at the outset. The best speeches come only after many, many re-writes.

6. **Put Your Own Spin On The Material.** You may block your creative juices if you think everything you say has to be original. Don't worry about being unique, just put your personal spin on it. The audience wants to hear your personal point of view.

7. **Make Only Three Main Points.** It is always tempting to tell as much as you can about a subject, but this will confuse and overwhelm your audience. Keep your major points to three and your audience will find it easier to follow your speech organisation.

8. **Craft A Take-away Line.** When people can't make a speaker's session, they ask others who were there, "What did the speaker talk about?" What they say you said is your take-away line. You'd like people to walk out with that nugget.

9. **Decide The Minimum Your Audience Needs To Know.** What is the very least the audience needs to know about your topic? What is the most critical? Leave out material that would be "nice to know". You probably won't have time for it anyhow.
10. **Write Using the principle:** "What's In It For Me?" People are really only interested in material that affects them.

NOTE:
 1. Write As If You Are Conversing With One Person.
 2. Decide What You Want Your Audience To Do Or Think Differently As A Result Of Your Speech.
 3. Use "Audience-Involvement" Devices.

Preparation

1. Read yourself full
   a. Give your audience something solid. This means work. Get moving by filling your mind with the latest and the best.
   b. Go to the nearest suitable library. Pull out all the books that you feel may have something on the subject. Then look at the index of each book. Read the relevant pages and those only of the other books. You can quickly gather, when you are *looking for something specific*.

2. Think yourself clear
   a. Picture audience. What do you really wish to say to it? Every talk should have only one, two or three major points (thrusts). You should be able to state the whole message of your talk in one sentence.

3. Make yourself interesting
   a. Use example, comparisons.
   b. So go from things to ideas, not ideas to things. Then people will stay awake and follow you.

How to Structure Your Talk

A good talk should have 3 parts:
1. *Introduction*.
   An indication of the structure (major points or divisions) of your talk.
2. The *body* of your talk (major points or arguments).
3. *Conclusion*. Don't neglect the *Second* of these parts: a statement of the *structure* of your talk, i.e. a map of where you're going. Unfortunately, many speakers do.

1. *Introduction:* You might start with a story or incident that engages the attention and interest of the audience.
2. An indication of the structure of your talk is a must.
   A. The Body of your talk is important.
3. *Conclusion:* You summarise your arguments and perhaps return to the story or incident you began with to do so.

Be Precise and to the Point

Write to the point and simple. Do not think that using pompous vocabulary will make you super cool. This is not the case. This is in fact lower the chances of one reading the article.

Justify Yourself

Every point that you make in your piece should have a reason. It is important to justify whatever you say. This adds support to your perspective, be it an argument.

Vocabulary

Avoid Unnecessary Repetition and Word Clutter

Do not repeat words just to catch up with the word limit. This will diminish the attractiveness of your article. Try and use different words to make it look more interesting and appealing.

Omit Incomprehensible Word Clouts

Do not use a bunch of words to explain what can simply be stated. This shows that the writer is trying to fill out spaces and makes the reader lose interest.

Cut Down on Felicitous Phrases

Set up cognizance of exaggerated language. Watch out for fancy words and cut them down.

Cut Down the Urge to Use Colloquialisms Excessively

While writing, it is a very strong temptation to express yourself with the new buzz words, slang and jargon to give your write-up a cool uplift. While this can rock for some readers, the method would never let you produce a seasoned article.

Grammar and Punctuation Guide

Grammar is one of the most important factors one needs to consider in order to **improve your writing**. Try to express things comprehensively.

Watch Out for Those Tenses

Do not change tenses within sentences. Incorrect use of tenses makes a negative impression of the writer. Understand and practice the basic rules of grammar to improvise on your writing.

Avoid Passive Sentences

Passive sentences are to be avoided. Passivity makes for fragile, unappealing writing.

Go Slow on Adverbs

Instead of using adverbs for your copy, try to be elaborative by experimenting with different words, phrases and synonyms.

Editing Tips

Good editing, like good writing, is a skill that cannot be taught. Practice and time is what makes you well at it. Editing can make your work more lively, valuable and in due course more prone to be read.

Take Your Time

Editing takes time, so do not expect to get done in a short span of time.

Proofread

Reread your article to pick up any stupid mistakes that you might have made.

Draft and Edit

Do not assume that the first draft that you write will eventually be the final one. Make it a habit to write at least two to three drafts. This will help you encounter mistakes and will also help you speed up while writing.

Always Remember the Spell Check

Nothing makes a bad impression than typos, misspelling errors and wrong choice of words. Always give your copy a last spell check to avoid the bad taste.

Copy Writing

Advertising and **marketing** are twins; two robust pillars standing tall to support the same objective – get the sales going and the cash flowing in.

Advertising Copy Model

The main objective for inking an **advertising copy** in the first place is to get the customer to act; to buy from you. You are a salesperson in pursuit of customers to convince. Remember, there is no one universal law that dictates the success of an advertising copy. Various experts and professionals from the advertising realm have their own opinions and approaches.

8 Tips for Writing an Effective Advertising Copy

1. Determine what is it that you're working to sell. Remember, it's not the product that consumers buy; it's the set of benefits and advantages that are associated

with the product. Start off by determining the stance you will be adopting with reference to your product and/or service.
2. The next is to get your word choice right because it's not just "what you say"; it's also "how you say it". Your tonality, attitude and energy will be relayed through the words you select for the advertising copy.
3. Incorporate easy words and short length sentences. Experts cite the ideal average sentence length to be between 17-20 words; longer sentences tend to leave the customer behind and lost. Don't bother selecting ideas that you can't reduce to lesser phrases yourself.
4. Anyone who can take his or her ideas, translate them into the common man's lingo and have it come across as persuasive.
5. Honesty is the best policy. Customers are not dumb and they definitely don't want to be perceived so either; no free rides here. Don't exaggerate or blow up facts; present them as they are in refined language.
6. "Speak" to the customer through your word arrangement & choice. Ensure you come across as if talking directly to the customer. Being passive & using the third person doesn't work too well in advertising copies; be active, bring the first person into play and utilise action verbs.
7. Be a leader.
8. Take time out to read the piece multiple times. Once doesn't do the trick; review it 2-3 times. You'll be surprised to see how easily mistakes can escape your eyes in the first go.

Copywriting Tip: What's the Difference Between Professional and Effective Copy?

How to Write Tight – Self-editing Tips to Make Your Manuscript Ready for Publication

As writers, we hear it all the time. We need to "write tight," which just means we need to trim all the flab from our manuscripts and make every word count.

Here are some self-editing tips that will help you "write tight" and take your manuscripts from flabby to fit for publication in no time!

1. **Avoid a lot of back story** - information about the POV character's history and background. Weave all this into the story instead of loading the manuscript down with too many sentences or paragraphs of straight narrative before the action begins.
2. **Simplify your sentences wherever possible.** Watch for redundant or unnecessary phrases. As writers, we need to "show, not tell" as often as possible. Yet, some writers tend to show and then tell the same information, which is redundant. Watch out for this in your manuscripts. Also, look for the redundant phrases below and others like them.

Stand up	=	stand
Sit down	=	sit
Turned back	=	turned
Turned around	=	turned
He thought to himself	=	He thought.
She shrugged her shoulders	=	she shrugged
She whispered softly	=	she whispered
He nodded his head	=	he nodded

3. **Avoid adverbs for the most part.** Use strong, descriptive verbs instead.
   Flabby: She smiled slightly at the photographer.
   Fit: She grinned at the photographer.
4. **Avoid using the same word over and over in a paragraph.** Go back and reread each sentence. Have you repeated the same word several times within a single sentence or paragraph? If so, substitute another word with the same meaning.
5. **Don't overuse names.** Beginning writers tend to have the characters address each other by name too often. When you speak to a friend, you don't constantly say his name. Don't have your characters do this either. It doesn't ring true, and it draws the reader OUT of the story.
6. **Limit the description in a dialogue tag.** Again, beginning writers tend to load down the dialogue tags (the "he said, she said," part of the dialogue) with too many details. If you must describe what a character is doing as he says something, put that information in a separate sentence, not in the dialogue tag. And keep it short.
7. **Avoid participle phrases** - particularly at the beginning of sentences. Participle phrases end in the letters -ing. Go back over every page of your manuscript and circle the places where you've started a sentence with a participle phrase. If your manuscript is loaded down with participle phrases it tends to distract the reader and pull him out of the story.
8. **No idle chit-chat.** Be sure the dialogue advances the storyline. Readers don't need to hear the characters talking about anything that doesn't somehow relate

directly to what's happened so far or what will happen next or later in the story.

9. **Minimise use of the passive voice.** Here's an example of passive voice: The ball was hit by Tina. Here's the same information in active voice: Tina hit the ball.

10. **Use active, descriptive verbs.**
    Flabby: I was the one who made the decision to go home.
    Fit: I decided to go home.
    Strengthen weak verbs. You can usually eliminate *was* and *were* by replacing them with stronger, more descriptive verbs. Usually, *was* and *were* precede an -ing word, and you can change the -ing word to make it stronger.
    Flabby: He was talking to my brother.
    Fit: He talked to my brother.

11. **Minimise use of the verb "to be" to keep the word count down.**
    Flabby: She is a graceful dancer.
    Fit: She dances gracefully.

12. **Cut the verb preceding an infinitive if it's not needed.**
    Flabby: She was able to fix the bicycle.
    Fit: She fixed the bicycle.

13. **Avoid using the word that when you don't need it.**
    Re-read each sentence that includes that, then read the sentence without that. If it sounds all right without it, cut it.

    Also, avoid other words we tend to rely on yet don't add much to the story. The word suddenly should be used as infrequently as possible. Otherwise, it tends to sound as if your characters are constantly jumping around.

14. **Watch for pet words or phrases you tend to favor without even realising it.** Common words like then, as, and when tend to get over used often.
15. **Avoid stall phrases that slow down the action for no good reason.** Phrases such as: *tried to*, *began to* and *started to* can be changed to the simple past tense of the verb.

Dramatic Dialogue TIPS

Dramatic dialogue breathes life into a story.

#1: Writing Dialogue

Dialogue in a story is different from real-life talk. If we were to record a normal conversation we'd find it filled with idle chatter, incomplete thoughts and broken sentences. Most real-life conversations would be too tedious to read.

Written dialogue has to capture and hold the attention of readers. If your characters ramble on, the way people do in real life, you'll lose your audience. So cut out the flab: words that don't serve any useful purpose, sentences and paragraphs that cause the story to drag.

#2: Writing Good Dialogue

Effective dialogue is not an exact reproduction of real-life speech but rather a condensed form that cuts out verbiage while retaining the flavour of authentic, natural speech.

Good dialogue imitates the natural rhythms of everyday speech; it contains nuances, overtones and original turns of phrase that bring out the individual personalities of characters.

#3: Purposeful, Dynamic Dialogues

Good writers manipulate dialogue to achieve an intended effect; for example to:

a. Reveal character or motives
b. Individualise speakers
c. Convey important information
d. Highlight crucial moments or build suspense
e. Move the action forward

#4: How to Write Dialogue that Illuminates Character

With dialogue you're letting your characters speak for themselves; you're showing their personalities, motivations and feelings.

Narration keeps readers at a distance, dialogue allows them to identify and feel with your characters.

#5: Conversation Dialogue Differentiates Characters

Give your characters their own distinctive voices. As in real life, the differences in diction, nuances and speech patterns will differentiate your characters and reflect their individual personalities. This contrast in voices also adds to the dramatic tension in the story.

#6: Dialect in Conversation Dialogue

With dialect, a little goes a long way. You don't want to put readers off with strings of unintelligible words. Just a light touch will do - a few well-chosen phrases to bring out the flavour of the dialect.

#7: Dramatic Dialogue Conveys Critical Information

Use dialogue to convey important information in an interesting way. Short paragraphs of dialogue, in which characters ask and give information, are easier to read than long narratives.

Dramatise the dialogue; inject feeling into the giver and receiver of the information. Build suspense by having the speaker withhold the information or delay giving it. Like this:

"Were any other lives lost?"

"No - perhaps it would have been better if there had."

"What do you mean?"

#8: Dramatic Dialogue Highlights Crucial Moments and Builds Suspense

Dialogue dramatises: it creates living scenes, taking readers right into the thick of the action. The way characters speak - what they say or leave unsaid - lend an air of excitement, even a sense of mystery, to the story.

#9: Dynamic Dialogue Moves the Plot Forward

Dialogue moves the action forward quickly. What would take a long passage of narration to describe can be accomplished in fewer words and with greater impact through dialogue.

#10: Dramatic Dialogue Makes Sparks Fly

Think of your story in terms of a stage performance: how do your characters sound? Choose words for their dramatic impact: their emotional overtones, imagery, sound and rhythm.

#11: Reader-Friendly Dialogue

Keep dialogues short and to the point. Begin a new paragraph each time a different character starts to speak. Short paragraphs create lots of white space and make the page look more inviting to readers.

Avoid long speeches; they pack a page with type and make it difficult to read as there is no rest for the eyes.

If you're tempted to write long passages of dialogue, ask yourself whether the story really needs it. Most of the time, the writing can be condensed. On the rare occasion when a long speech is absolutely necessary, break it up into short paragraphs interposed with narrative or with another character asking questions or offering comments.

#12: Mixing Dialogue and Narration

Dialogue on its own does not always give the complete picture; stories also need narration to round out the scenes. Use narration to describe and explain characters and their actions.

Create dramatic tension with the right balance of dialogue and narration.

Academic Writing

Writing is *communicating*. Good writing helps your reader understand your ideas as clearly as possible. How to make the task of writing easier in English assignments?

1. Whenever possible, write on subjects that actually interest you.
2. Write on subjects that you know about or want to know about.

3. Before you begin to write a draft, explore your ideas freely with the help of invention techniques.
4. Have an idea of the audience you are writing for, and keep that person or group of people in your mind as you write.
5. Decide what your purpose is and what you want your writing to accomplish. Will it inform? Persuade? Entertain? Will it help you discover your own ideas?
6. Don't worry about details in your first draft. Try just to get your ideas down on paper. You can shape your ideas later.
7. Reread your own writing frequently. Try to read objectively, as though you were not the author and you were seeing it for the first time.
8. Let others read what you have written and give you feedback.
9. Don't be afraid to add, delete, or move your ideas around.
10. Once your ideas are on paper, check the grammar, vocabulary, spelling, and punctuation to make the writing as correct as you can.

Fundamentals of Layout

A layout is a plan or blueprint for design structure.

What is layout?

In our context, layout is the arrangement of design elements on paper.

These elements are- pictures, types, graphic shapes and colours.

PICTURES include drawings, photographs, charts, graphs, maps etc

- Headlines and text matter are formed by TYPES
- Patterns, lines and areas filled with colour and tone make GRAPHICS

The main purpose of this exercise is to lay them out in a pleasing functional order

Layout Terminology

- Advertising layout - a plan for an advertisement
- Press layout - for a newspaper
- Page layout - page for magazine pages
- Dummy - complete compilation of all pages
- Make-up - process of putting together the elements of a newspaper page
- Mock-up - The prototype of an exhibition stall
- Storyboard - ideas presented or simulated visually, such as film, TV or web page, visual presentation begins in the form of layouts called STORYBOARD (A storyboard is a series of related pictures depicting what the action might be in the actual film when it is finally produced or the website is finally launched.

Who can make a layout?

Printers and DTP operators.

Graphic Design

GRAPHIC DESIGN is the application of type, colour and images on a surface to create a clear and effective whole.

- Graphic designs are made to break communication barriers.
- The TYPES are arranged to make the composition legible without too much strain

- COLOURS are chosen not for themselves but to enhance the message and create the right atmosphere
- VISUALS are combined with types and manipulated and sized to capture and hold attention
- DESIGN also includes putting all these elements in oreder-arranging them into logical sequence
- THE PLAN OF A GRAPHIC DESIGN IS LAYOUT

Types of Layout

Basically 4 kinds of layout
1. ROUGH LAYOUT
2. ARTWORK
3. CONVENTIONAL LAYOUT
4. DIGITAL LAYOUT

1. Rough Layout

- Rough layout is mainly used for presentation.
- It is also used as a printer's guide.

There are two types of rough layouts:

A. Working Rough: Made for the benefit of the technical staff mainly – photographers, printers, designers, artists etc

B. Finished Rough: Is a close approximation of its final from. It presents all the elements of type, colour, picture and accurately in regard to by size, style, spacing placement etc

2. Artwork Layout

- Rough layout is finally converted into artwork for the printer

- It is usually in black and white format.
- Here all the elements of the page – like area for illustration, graphic shape and colour – are made into outlines and typed out as line art.

3. Conventional Layout

- Here display type (heading and sub-heading) is lettered in, and visuals are sketched in the same size and tone as in the final product.
- Text copy or reading matter is indicated by a copy-block
- Height of an article is denoted by an 'x'.

4. Digital Layout

- In digital layout, the illustrative matter is scanned and finished by software like Photoshop, CorelDraw and Illustrator
- Before you scan, determine the quality requirement of your layout and choose correct resolution.

Adverts, Brochures, Sales Literature, Reports

Writing letters, reports, notes and other communications are important skills for business and personal life. Good letters help to get results, where poor letters fail. People judge others on the quality of their writing, so it's helpful to write well. Here are some simple tips for writing letters and communications of all sorts.

Generally, whatever you are writing, get to the main point, quickly and simply. Avoid lengthy preambles. Don't spend ages setting the scene or explaining the background, etc.

If you are selling, promoting, proposing something you must identify the main issue (if selling, the strongest unique perceived benefit) and make that the sole focus. Introducing other points distracts and confuses the reader.

Use language that your reader uses. If you want clues as to what this might be imagine the newspaper they read, and limit your vocabulary to that found in the newspaper.

Avoid obvious grammatical errors, especially inserting single apostrophes where incorrect, which irritates many people and which is seen by some to indicate a poor education.

Probably the best rule for safe use of apostrophes is to restrict their use simply to possessive (e.g., girl's book, group's aims) and missing letters in words (e.g. I'm, you're, we've).

Writing Reports – Template Structure

Typical structure template for writing a report:

- Title, author, date.
- Contents.
- Introduction and Terms of Reference (or aims/scope for report).
- Executive Summary (1-2 pages maximum) containing main points of **evidence**, **recommendations** and **outcomes**.
- **Background**/history/**situation**.
- **Implications/issues/opportunities/threats**, with **source-referenced** facts and figures **evidence**.

- **Solution**/action/decision **options** with implications/effects/results, including **financials** and parameters **inputs and outputs**.
- **Recommendations and actions** with **input and outcomes values and costs**, and if necessary **return on investment**.
- Appendices.
- Optional Bibliography and Acknowledgements.

Map out your structure before you begin researching and writing your report.

Ensure the purpose, aims and scope of the report are clearly explained in your terms of reference.

The executive summary should be very concise, summarising the main recommendations and findings. Provide interpretation of situations and options. Show the important hard facts and figures. Your recommendations should include implications, with values and costs where applicable. Unless yours is a highly complex study, limit the executive summary to less than two sides of standard business paper.

The body of the report should be divided into logical sections. The content must be very concise. Use hard facts and figures, evidence and justification. Use efficient language - big reports with too many words are not impressive. The best reports are simple and quick to read because the writer has properly interpreted the data and developed viable recommendations.

Do not cram lots of detail, diagrams, figures, evidence, references etc., into the main body of the report. Index and attach these references as appendices at the end of the report.

Where you state figures or evidence you must always identify the source.

Show figures in columns. Try to support important figures with a graph.

If it's appropriate to acknowledge contributors then do so in the introduction or a separate section at the end.

Editing Your Manuscript: 6 Tips

1. **Check your manuscript for flow and clarity.**
   Be sure that your text is logical and you finish thoughts. Explain or elaborate on any words, thoughts, or phrases that your audience might not be familiar with.
2. **Don't vary your style.**
   Make sure that you use commas in the same way and make your capitalisation (of pronouns for deity, titles, names, etc.) consistent throughout the manuscript.
3. **Avoid repetition.**
   Weed out repetitive sentences, thoughts, and paragraphs.
4. **Use the spelling and grammar check** in your word processing program.
   This helpful tool will catch major mistakes. However, don't simply make all of the program's suggested changes, as it will often cause you to make errors. For example, it might tell you to make something singular or plural that should not be or tell you that a full sentence is a fragment or tell you to use "me" when you should use "I."
5. **Find out if your publishing company uses specific style or submission guidelines** or style manuals as a standard for editing and formatting.

6. **Never underestimate the importance of a professional edit.**
   Even the most trained eye can miss things, so having a professional editor team up with you and work on your manuscript is invaluable.

The Best Way to Learn To Write is by Writing